Everyone Wants Your Money

Helping You Navigate Through Philanthropy

Gray Keller

authorHOUSE®

AuthorHouse™
1663 Liberty Drive
Bloomington, IN 47403
www.authorhouse.com
Phone: 1-800-839-8640

First published by AuthorHouse 10/29/2010

ISBN: 978-1-4520-3755-4 (e)
ISBN: 978-1-4520-3754-7 (sc)
ISBN: 978-1-4520-3753-0 (hc)

Library of Congress Control Number: 2010908596

Printed in the United States of America

This book is printed on acid-free paper.

To everyone who wants to make a difference
by being a blessing

CONTENTS

ACKNOWLEDGEMENTS

Only a life lived for others is a life worthwhile.
—Albert Einstein

I WANT TO THANK THE School of Global Leadership and Entrepreneurship at Regent University, and especially Dr. Jay Gary, who helped me think through so many issues pertaining to philanthropy, leadership, and futuring. I also want to thank Dr. Paul Schervish, director of the Center on Wealth and Philanthropy at Boston College, for taking his time to dialogue with me in regard to the spirituality of philanthropy. A special thank you to the former Head of Global Philanthropy Services for UBS Switzerland, Dr. Maximilian Martin for sharing thoughts about strategic philanthropy.

My gratitude and appreciation to all my friends and family who have given their prayers, words of encouragement, and love to me over the course of this research project—thank you. I also want to thank all of the nonprofits, private foundations, and other philanthropic leaders that I've worked alongside—you have enriched my thinking and life more than you will ever know. My heart is forever grateful to Gary Haugen for opening my eyes and heart to the extreme poor and oppressed widows, orphans, and sexually exploited children of the world. Your work is the reason why I continue to press on as a philanthropic leader. I want to thank Danita's Children for allowing me the privilege of loving and being with the beautiful orphans after the horrific earthquake in Haiti. You and your organization are truly doing the work of philanthropy. From everyone who has read manuscripts upon manuscripts of this work, thank you. Thank you for your feedback, wisdom, and editorial skills in shaping this work. A special thank you to Michelle Williamson who volunteered her time, energy, and expertise in editing, reading and working with my manuscript. Also, I want to thank Krystal Perea and Jules Polachek for your input and editorial pizzazz.

Finally, I want to give a most special thank you to my wife, Dixie, who gave me the time (i.e., years) to focus on this project. Thank you for your support, encouragement, prayers, and love. Thank you for allowing me to travel the world to research philanthropic initiatives. Thank you for being a philanthropic leader with me through life. Thank you for making a difference by being a blessing.

INTRODUCTION

To give money away is an easy matter and in any man's power. But to decide to whom to give it, and how large and when, and for what purpose and how, is neither in every man's power nor an easy matter.
—Aristotle

PHILANTHROPIC LEADERSHIP COMBINES THE STUDY and practice of leadership with the field of philanthropy. Now more than ever, the field of philanthropy needs leadership. The majority of charities and foundations continue to approach philanthropic endeavors with good hearts, but they often lack the necessary leadership required for accountability, sustainability, and measurable human flourishing. Celebrities from Bono to Oprah, major philanthropists like Bill Gates and Warren Buffett, and political leaders from Bill Clinton to George H. Bush bring new excitement, awareness, and energy to the needs of philanthropy. But if we are not careful, philanthropic leaders will repeat the same mistakes of our forefathers, namely spending over $2 trillion on foreign aid with little to no improvement. In the spring of 2006, Eric Thurman, CEO of Geneva Global writes in *Harvard International Review*, "the problem with philanthropy today is that too much attention is focused on counting receipts and too little on outcomes."[1]

This practice continues in all spheres of charity and philanthropic activity. After many generous givers in America were quick to give to the Hurricane Katrina Fund, today much of the devastation of New Orleans and the Gulf Coast remains. Giving money without proper leadership produces the type of results our global society has witnessed. From places like Africa and India where billions upon billions of foreign aid and charity have been given, these areas remain, for the most part, as if aid has never reached their shores.

Unfortunately, compassionate well-meaning philanthropists, missionaries and non-government organizations often believe the problem of philanthropic concerns is a lack of funding, or the continual never-ending need to raise more money. The problem is not a lack of funding, but rather a lack of meaningful, well thought-out, strategic philanthropic leadership. The hope of this book is to stimulate the thought and practice of donors like you, to reconsider how you give, why you give, and what you want to see as a result of your own philanthropic leadership.

This book is not a typical "how-to" do a, b, and c to ensure enduring success. The majority of newly published books on leadership, business, finance, and management speak mostly on how to make money, cut costs, generate wealth, and retire young and rich. In my pursuit to find new research on leadership and philanthropy, few if any books synergize both topics in a straightforward applied way. This book will not give you the secret of how to raise more cash for your next fundraising event, nor will this book instruct you on how to start a 501 (c) 3, or run your board. Literature abounds on those topics. This book is not about corporate social responsibility (CSR) or the best practices of micro-financing in the developing world.

This book asks one primary question: in regard to philanthropy, what does it take to make a positive difference in the lives of others? In a word, leadership is the difference between whether a charitable organization succeeds or fails. A second question quickly follows the first: what type of leadership is needed to make a difference in the world of philanthropy? With a slew of leadership theories and styles up for grabs, the art of giving money away for philanthropic purposes does not lend itself to just any leadership practice. Different situations and different foundations and causes, both here and abroad, will need different leadership at different times. However, when you, the donor, become aware of your own leadership style, your own values and beliefs, and your passion for making a difference in the lives of others, then through intentional practice, you will become a philanthropic leader.

This book presents a new perspective for developing high net worth donors as philanthropic leaders. It challenges the donor-leader to go above and beyond the traditional thought and practice of philanthropy: writing checks, out bidding friends at auctions, and maintaining a private foundation. A dynamic relationship should exist at the very core of philanthropy. The Greek etymology for philanthropy is "love for mankind." Love for another person is at the heart and soul of philanthropy. When the focus of philanthropic activity is only centered on money, the community at large suffers. Even though fundraising and money typify a great deal of philanthropic activity, leadership is not primarily about money. Leadership is about the relationship the leader has with his or her followers. Leadership is being responsible for the decisions you make for others. Philanthropic leadership concerns itself with responsible decision making while realizing the importance of relationship. When the relationship between the leader and follower, or the donor and the recipient, is only around the exchange of money, then the relationship often dwindles as does the money. At the end of the day, you are not a bank. If people only want your money, then a bank is where you should point them. Mostly, when donor fatigue and fund raising fatigue begin to set in, when the pressure to increase last year's budget arrives, and when you face the many demands life creates, then the bar of leadership must be raised to a higher level of insight, wisdom and purpose.

This book also looks at the hard realities of philanthropy. What happens when money is mishandled, expectations are not met, and goodwill becomes a disguise for greed, power and prestige? Many high net worth donors no longer give with great expectations or they have simply stopped giving all together. The ugly side of philanthropy is not only dangerous, but it exists in more places and organizations than you probably would ever imagine or believe. Yet the future of philanthropy, for donors in particular, does not need to be ugly, unethical, or blindsided by the many harsh realities of giving. With philanthropic leadership you will become the donor with a mission, strategy and heart aligned for purpose, progress and positive change. You will know how to say no and make your yes truly significant as you lead from your total being and not simply from your bank account. You will lead with clarity as you understand your own values and beliefs, and you will better shape the future by giving strategically where results count.

This book is based on many years of research as well as real-world positive and negative experiences of charitable giving. I have had the privilege and responsibility of not only giving away millions of dollars to charitable organizations, churches and missions, but also of thinking, reflecting and engaging other high net worth donors on both the burdens and blessings of giving. If you have spent any time personally reflecting upon your own philanthropic experiences, this book will help you relate to the challenges and opportunities of giving wisely. This book provides you with new tools, insights and strategies to help you perform better as a donor, feel better as a donor and have greater alignment between who you are and how you lead as a donor. As a result, you will experience a greater love for giving, because you will be aware of who you are not only as a donor-leader, but also as a member of society who truly cares to make a difference in the lives of others.

Learning the Philanthropic Leadership philosophy ultimately consists of how you relate to others, your money, and life. It also examines what you believe about people, money, and life. It interrogates ideas, strategies, and the notion that money is the answer to the world's greatest problems. Finally, you discover your giftedness, values, and beliefs and how you desire to lead as a change agent. This book presupposes that leadership is learned both from a principle/theoretical perspective and also from a holistic participatory worldview of living and leading others in relationship for a common cause.

Ultimately, philanthropic leadership begins with you in relation with another person. It is not about how wealthy you are, how much money you have given, or even how much money you hope to leave one day. Philanthropic leadership is leading from your unique sense of purpose with authenticity, integrity, and innovation. It is leading, living, and giving wisely, strategically and intentionally. Philanthropic leadership ultimately is not about the legacy you leave, but rather the leadership you give.

Leading your legacy now rather than hoping you have left one once you are gone is essential to how you relate to others, ideas, and eternity.

For too long donors have continued to follow the crowd, insisting on doing business as usual, while never fully understanding the *whys* behind their actions. Another black-tie gala, another live auction prize, another mission trip to Africa, another walk-a-thon, and life continues on. Yet, when donors lead beyond the conventional future, they begin to get excited about the counter future of giving. The counter future reacts against the never-ending need of raising funds for projects and administrative costs. Rather, the counter future sells products as portrayed with organizations participating under the Product (RED) umbrella. The counter future asks, "Why should not the wealthy nations of the West simply forgive debt to those developing countries, which cannot arise out of extreme poverty as a result of the many complexities that keep them in bondage?" And even when philanthropic leaders like Bono appeal to the United States for debt relief for countries in Africa, the counter reactions to the conventional wisdom of the past leaves people still desperate for more innovative ways of thinking and leading philanthropic missions.

This is where the creative future brings new ideas from all worlds of thought. From the banking world of finance, to the vast spectrum of religious views about charity, to the marketplace of social entrepreneurs, a holistic dimension of creativity emerges when we listen to the leading known minds of the world and the ideas from the heart and soul of the widow, the orphan, and the poor and oppressed about how to bring real transformation to philanthropy's biggest and most crucial needs. The poorest of the poor and some of the wealthiest people in the world need to come together in love for purposes greater than their own agendas to listen and learn. When world religious leaders, both living and dead, have something to say about philanthropic leadership, then donors need to listen. If it be from leaders like Muhammad Yunus (Islam), Mother Teresa (Catholic), Jesus of Nazareth (Judaism), and a pluralistic stream of other thinkers ranging from Aristotle to the Tao who speaks to the world's greatest needs, then the donor-leader should listen. Philanthropic leaders must learn to listen to orphans in India, widows in Africa, children in the inner cities of America, and all of the other voices calling out in the wilderness for help. Then and only then, will philanthropic leaders begin to learn the wisdom of those who seem so helpless on the surface, but have hope and incredible insight to make a difference.

Even if you do not agree with Bill Clinton's political views, you can learn from his insights on giving. If you are a Christian, then you can learn valuable wisdom from someone like Muhammad Yunus and apply his thinking to your organization. Hence, as a philanthropic leader you are about to enter upon a lifelong journey of learning, listening, thinking, and leading. Great leaders know how to wrestle with ideas that are not their own. They simply do not throw out the baby because the bath water is at a different temperature. They learn the art of seeing problems and issues from multiple perspectives, while realizing there is great power in paradoxical action. Life is not all black and white, clean and neat, right and wrong, and neither is your leadership. Learning to lead with tensions, paradoxical ideas, and even at times, without having the answers, your philanthropic leadership will begin to mature, grow, and develop into far reaching depths beyond the band-aid solutions of pop culture. It will require wisdom tempered with courage, hope and faith in alignment with sound thinking, and selfless love empowering those you seek to serve. Philanthropic leadership requires a new order of living.

Money Is Not the Answer

Nothing is more dangerous or difficult than
introducing a new order of things.
—The Prince

When it comes to philanthropy, money is not the answer. The more money thrown at an issue typically creates a bigger problem. The United States government believes money is the answer. In recent days, Congress passed a bill exceeding $750 billion (of your money) to companies and organizations whose track record is arguably criminal at worst and poor at best. Sadly, the news media continues to report that Congress needs more money to bailout more companies in this current economic crisis. Is throwing more money at bad debt, poorly operating companies, and pitiful leadership the best solution? Would you continue to give your teenagers more money every time they asked without question, purchase them a new car again and again, and continue to support their lifestyle as they attempt to keep up with the Paris Hiltons of the world? Unfortunately, there are many parents who do, and likewise, many nonprofit organizations that think, dream, hope and believe just like Congress or the teenager next door: "I'm entitled to your money without question or reservation, period." Why? "Because I know how to help the needy better than you do," they make you believe. Just the other day, as this current economic crisis is occurring, I attended a board meeting of a nonprofit public charity, who claimed they had already given away more money than they had in scholarship funds and that they would need to raise more money because the needs would become greater as a result of the economy at large. Not one board member asked, "How can we give away money that we do not have?" and "how can we think we can generate even more money when donor giving is down?" This particular organization, like many nonprofits, believes it cannot turn away anyone because of a lack of money. And this is clearly one of the problems America is currently facing. From home loans to car loans, "no money down," and "no payments till next year" continues to be the motto, slogan, and mantra from Christmas catalogues to everyday marketing. This systemic ideology of entitlement without responsibility and accountability must stop, and a new order of ideas must emerge.

In his book, Lee Iacocca asks, "Where Have all the Leaders Gone?" In the nonprofit world, many of them have stopped leading because of the demands of raising funds. As numerous men and women excel in their field of expertise, they often find themselves promoted to the executive director, president, or Chief Executive Officer (CEO) of a particular foundation, nonprofit, or charity. Many times, these leaders get promoted not based on their fundraising skills, their administrative skills, or their visionary capabilities, but rather because they do what they do with excellence. Yet once they find themselves at the head of the helm, they are no longer allowed to do what they love. They begin to take on a new mission. Now they are the voice and the face of their organization. From speaking all over the nation and world and connecting with high net worth donors in attempting to feed the beast, these newly executive directors have truly become nothing more than fundraisers. And the assumption is that the beast only likes to eat money. As Machiavelli claimed, "Nothing is more dangerous or difficult than introducing a new order of things." In this book, I challenge you not to do business as usual, not to give blindly, but to take leadership over your philanthropy and to rethink and lead differently.

Leaders are not fundraisers. Leaders lead. Fundraisers, on the other hand, raise funds. When the leader of an organization spends the majority of his or her time raising funds, then he or she should step down from his or her position of president, executive director, or whatever leadership position he or she holds and take on the job and responsibly of a fundraiser. Similarly, the philanthropic leader is primarily not about raising funds. The philanthropic leader may give his or her money to a charity or cause, but this too is not the primary purpose of the donor-leader.

CHARITY IS NOT THE ANSWER

> *Charity is injurious unless it helps the recipient*
> *to become independent of it.*
> —John D. Rockefeller

A new order of things, ideas, and philanthropic leaders is slowly emerging. Within this new movement is the understanding that giving money rarely fixes any major philanthropic problem. Yes, there will always be a place and need for charity in society; however, charity is the giving to others without expecting anything in return. For example, if and when you have ever given money to a homeless person from your car window at the busy intersection of your town, then you have practiced charity. You have given money to someone you do not know, in hopes that he or she will use it for good. But you do not follow up, you do not measure the results, you do not see if the person truly bought that train ticket to his or her long lost aunt's house or if he or she used your charity to simply purchase more booze. The point of helping was primarily given because you saw a need and felt compelled for whatever reasons to be charitable.

This book is not about charity. Charity, or giving alms, is an enormous business in America and around the world. By practicing the continuation of giving alms without strategic leadership, thought, and foresight often creates more burdens than blessings. Charity creates dependency from handouts along with a sense of entitlement that often reinforces apathy for the recipient. Within this dependency comes a power dynamic for the donor. The donor has the power to give or not to give. The donor has the power of when to give. The donor has the power of how much to give. Charity ultimately empowers the donor, while causing the recipient to remain at the mercy seat of the powerful. This type of power exploits the needy. It dehumanizes and removes dignity from their personhood, while creating more vulnerability and oppression especially in the developing world.

In addition, charity focuses time, effort, and one's intention on positioning to receive more rather than creating self-empowering products, services, and quality work to reduce or even eliminate the need for charity. Muhammad Yunus shows how handouts encourage people "to spend their energy and skill chasing 'free' things rather than using the same energy and skill to accomplish something on their own."[2] When the human heart focuses on getting more and more money, then it takes whatever it can, however it can. The temptation to steal, to cheat, and to use whatever means one can to corrupt the process of giving has been around for centuries and continues on today.

Corruption comes from both within and outside one's organization, foundation, or charity. The doors are open to board members, attorneys, accountants and consultants who understand how much money is at stake for granting oneself excessive fees, payments and bonuses before the actual charity goes to work. Newspaper headlines continue to shout the names of greedy leaders who drain foundations of money for their own lifestyles, while appearing to truly care for a particular cause. For example, CNBC's American Greed show is filled with stories like the con artist Raffaello Follieri who scammed everyone from Bill Clinton with the Clinton Foundation by promising to donate $50 million to other philanthropic leaders and organizations.[3] Nevertheless, corruption also comes externally through bribery, theft, and other forms of greed especially in the developing world.

To illustrate, the food brigade arrives to feed thousands upon thousands of widows, orphans, and children in Africa. Suddenly, the group is overcome by a band of rebels who take the food by force creating panic, oppression, and even death. Sometimes these rebel groups attempt to sell back the bags of rice and beans on the black market to make a profit for their own. All the while, this activity originated from your generous donation given in good faith thousands of miles away here in America. A nice picture of the children eating their food arrives in your mailbox, but the untold stories of children running for their lives, still starving to death, all because of the rebel forces continue with free reign.

In addition, when monies are wired around the world from your charity here in the United States to their on-site mission in the developing world, a nice charge occurs with the wire transfer from your generous donation. This is not necessarily corruption, but would it not be beneficial if all international financial institutions were to process free wire transfers to social nonprofit organizations, so that when your generous donation reaches the people it is intended to help, it is not all gone?

The free handout of charity also creates others problems. Economist William Easterly shares in his book, *The White Man's Burden*, how giving products like mosquito nets to prevent the spreading of malaria in Africa often become used for everything else from fishing nets to wedding veils. In other words, if the recipients are not instructed on the use of goods like mosquito nets, then what good is it to give these out? You may spend your good earned money on purchasing antiretroviral drugs to give to those who are suffering with Human Immunodeficiency Virus (HIV)/ Acquired Immune Deficiency Syndrome (AIDS), but if they do not have clean water to wash down those pills, then your money given to fix one problem leads to others.

Infrastructural problems from sanitation to clean water systems to education are only the beginning of a complexity of myriad issues and problems that quite frankly, all of the money in the world could not solve with your local dollar donation as you eat at Taco Bell. Although it is good to see fast food establishments like Taco Bell and other restaurants promoting world hunger initiatives, if we continue to believe that an extra dollar truly will save a life, then we are greatly deceived.

Many of the concerns plaguing the world consist of things that money simply cannot buy. Money cannot buy respect, dignity, inner spiritual peace, or lasting love. Yes, the giving of money is helpful and greatly needed, but it needs to be given, spent, invested, and saved wisely, strategically, and intentionally. At the end of the day, at the end of your philanthropic life, it is not so much how much you gave away, but rather how well you loved your neighbor whether he or she lived down the street from you, across town, or on the other side of the world.

In today's global society, philanthropic leadership looks beyond race, ethnicity, religion, creed, sex, or political ideology to love another for human flourishing. As a philanthropic leader, you will have to decide to give in a way that truly blesses another by bringing sustainable transformation and empowerment and place aside your own agenda and your own namesake. You will have to decide if you truly believe there is a better way of empowering charities to serve than simply giving money away. You will have to decide to take this life journey of philanthropic leadership to a deeper level of human connection and understanding instead of playing it safe behind the ivory tower of American philanthropy by adhering to the same established, ineffective rules of giving. The choice is yours, and I hope you join me, along with so many others around the globe who have become philanthropic leaders.

Chapter One:
Everyone Has a Story

Every one of us is a wonder. Every one of us has a story.
—Kristin Hunter

S TORIES ARE ANCHORS THAT CONNECT souls, establish relationships and keep the many passions, hopes, and dreams alive in those who share them. In philanthropy, for every donor who gives and for every recipient who receives there lies a story. A story of hope, a story of dreams fulfilled, and a story of fellow humans coming to the rescue of another is what philanthropy is all about. It is a story about love between people. One who has a need and another who delights to meet that need is the basic underlying story of philanthropy.

Love in action, love between two people, a leader and a follower, an initiator and a receiver, a person of strength being with a person of weakness continues to be told in the lives of people practicing philanthropic leadership all over the world. You have your story and I have mine, and each day that we have the privilege of living, we have the opportunity to live stories of blessings where love flourishes and empowers others to rise up and be a blessing themselves.

Throughout history we have the stories of those like Mother Teresa, who with a heart of love, held the dying, cared for the orphan, and exposed the great power of personal touch to those rejected by society. We have the stories of philanthropic leaders who blessed the alien widow as depicted in the book of *Ruth*. We have the story of Jesus telling how a poor widow gave more from her poverty than the rich from their wealth.

We have stories to challenge us to go deeper, to give greater, and to be better citizens of this world. We have stories to inspire and to learn from, to encourage and correct us, and to live forward by leading a life serving others. As we embark on the journey of what it means to become a philanthropic leader, allow me the opportunity to share with you my story.

MY STORY

> *The blessing of the Lord brings wealth, without painful toil for it.*
> —Proverbs 10:22

Several years ago, an advisor asked me how I would feel when I would become an instant multi-millionaire. His question struck me as odd because a few years prior I already felt like I was the wealthiest person living in Orlando, Florida. Even though at that time I was cleaning toilets, vacuuming floors, and doing other janitorial work as a graduate student, I felt alive, wealthy, and great!

For me, the feeling of wealth, of richness, did not come from hard work, inheritance, or winning the lottery. It came from a powerful thought that changed me: wealth occurs when all aspects of one's life remains in balance and proper perspective. Wealth is not about being financially rich in the eyes of the world. And it is not about having an American Express Centurion card (it is not perceived value). True wealth is knowing who you are as a person and living your life with integrity (it is real value). Or as the Apostle Paul once said, "Actually, I don't have a sense of needing anything personally. I've learned by now to be quite content whatever my circumstances. I'm just as happy with little as with much, with much as with little. I've found the recipe for being happy whether full or hungry, hands full or hands empty.

Whatever I have, whatever I am, I can make it through anything in the One who makes me who I am."[1]

For me, being wealthy meant being alive, living for a brighter tomorrow, and knowing that I am making a difference in the world. Wealth was not dependent upon my current financial circumstances. Being wealthy was a state of mind, a worldview system not based on materialism, but rather based on contentment, yet always striving ahead one day at a time. So the question caught me off guard, not so much because it was the wrong question to ask, but because I see the world, my life, and others differently.

LIFE PRINCIPLE: HOW YOU DEFINE WEALTH MATTERS

In the beginning of 2000, I decided to move to Orlando, Florida to pursue a Master's degree in Theology. Having graduated with a Bachelor's degree in philosophy, I thought that a Master's degree in theology would be the next logical step in my academic journey. But this time in my educational pursuits, I would be financially on my own. So with a car that was paid for, all of my personal belongings, and $600 I drove from Texas to Florida.

I met my future roommate over one or two phone conversations, never in person, and I was unsure about what awaited me in Orlando. After two long days on the road I finally arrived.

My life would never be the same.

I met my new roommate and a few of his friends as soon as I arrived. "Where is your bed? Do you have any furniture? What about a computer?" The questions were coming quickly. All I had was my car, some clothes, and a whole lot of faith. I did not have a computer. I did not have any furniture. I did not have a job, and I did not have a nice bank account to dip into. No trust funds, no savings and no future donors were on my radar.

That evening, my new roommate told me that he had seen a mattress in one of the dumpsters at the apartment complex earlier that day. So we went to the trash bin and carried the mattress to his apartment. The apartment

1 Philippians 4:11–13, the *Message*.

15

was his; I had not yet paid any money down to live there. So, my very first night in Orlando I slept in a sleeping bag on top of the mattress that we pulled out of the dumpster in an otherwise empty room. As I lay there, I thought, "Oh Lord, what in the world have I gotten myself into?"

Until this point in my life, I had lived rather well by the world's standards. This was the test of contentment that the Apostle Paul spoke of. Could I be happy living in such conditions without friends or family, a job and any sense of community or security? This was the question I kept asking myself. The temptation of wanderlust interrupted my thoughts and a whole list of "if onlys" came along: if only I had a lot of money, if only my parents would continue to support me, if only I had a long lost rich uncle who would surprise me with a check in the mail, if only I had the brashness to ask the wealthy for financial support, if only I could move into a brand-new apartment complex without a roommate and furnish it with my every wish.

I had to clear my mind of self-centered thoughts and figure out how I was going to make it on my own without going into debt. Being a poor graduate student is a great place to learn about contentment, debt management, giving, and the daily disciplines of living. I had a choice before me. I could either continue to look at everything I did not have, or learn to make it on my own in a way that was in step with my values.

LIFE PRINCIPLE: WHEN YOU RECEIVE, GIVE

A life lesson I learned early on as a teenager was simply not to go into debt. The small amount of debt I incurred during my college days was paid off within one year of sacrificial living and hard work. As a young child, I also learned the valuable lesson of giving, which I continue to practice to this day.

Each time I received something new, like a dress shirt for my birthday, I gave another shirt away. And when I purchased a new article of clothing, or whatever it may have been, I gave away any of my excess to others whom were truly needy. Once in college, I donated sweaters, shirts and other clothes to a Thanksgiving food and clothing drive. I remember to this day the surprise on the lady's face that processed my gifts of charity that year: "This is too nice," she said. "Are you sure you want to donate this to charity?" "Yes," I replied, knowing that I would have a fabulous Christmas and receive much more than the little amount that I gave.

These principles, values, and beliefs guided my actions and attitudes toward everything from materialism and accumulation, to charity and contentment. By committing to living these values out in my daily life, I already knew that I had more than the average person and that I could truly bless the life of another if I only gave and/or shared from what I had.

After living my values and beliefs in college, I was prepared to face challenges as a graduate student in Florida. I believed that acquiring debt for self-consumption, or asking others for money was intolerable. Ultimately, I believed I must think, act and live outside the box of traditional ways.

LIFE PRINCIPLE: GOD ANSWERS PRAYERS

I believed that God would supply all of my needs and much more if I would continue to look toward Him in faith and prayer. This belief came from my childhood and early youth when I saw God provide in my family's life. Having a history of seeing and believing worldly provisions come from the hand of God, I was in a better position to keep believing and trusting Him.

I prayed that He would bless me indeed beyond what anyone could ever think or imagine. And, over the past decade of my life, my prayers have been answered. With my very first job interview in Orlando, I was offered a part-time job on the spot working at a local shopping mall. This allowed me to begin paying my bills, while starting my graduate studies. Soon after, I made a short list of things that I needed: a lamp, a desk and chair, computer and printer, a real bed and a few other items. Within less than a month of praying for these specific items, each one was provided to me without money.

In addition, the pastor at my new church came up to me one Sunday and handed me a check for $1,000 that an individual had written on my behalf. By the time summer had rolled around, I met a group of guys who offered me a free room in a house as long as I would mow the lawn, clean dishes, and keep the house clean. Although this provision only lasted for the summer, it revealed God's hand of blessing. Then a new job arrived that introduced me to a couple who eventually offered me free room and board. This couple had spent years allowing both local students and foreign exchange students to stay in their home after their own children were grown and gone.

LIFE PRINCIPLE: LIVING YOUR PRINCIPLES, VALUES, AND BELIEFS MAKES A DIFFERENCE

Over the course of two and half years of working on my graduate degree, I was able to keep my living expenses minimal, while generating income. I did not have my every wish and desire, but I was able to continue a life of simplicity with generosity. By committing my life to a certain set of principles, values, and beliefs, I was able to be charitable on a small scale, while experiencing "the blessing of the Lord that brings wealth, without painful toil for it."

Through my own struggles of having plenty or being in want, I have lived a life where God's hand of blessing continues whether He gives or He takes away. As a result, I have had the opportunity to challenge assumptions about life, money, and work, while being free to think outside the box about some of the world's greatest philanthropic concerns.

This is only a portion of my story, a snapshot to provide you with insight into who I am, where I've come from, and why I think the way I do; your story does the same.

Understanding your story provides you with the framework of how you got to where you are in your life, why you make sense of the world the way you do, and how you can connect with others. Throughout the remainder of this book, I share different stories of philanthropic activity in hopes of enriching your understanding of what you will likely encounter as a philanthropic leader.

There are *Life Principles* scattered throughout the book to help focus your thoughts and to help you develop as a leader. The *Leadership Exercises* included at the end of each section are opportunities for you to immediately apply what you have just read to your leadership toolbox.

LEADERSHIP EXERCISE: YOUR STORY

For this exercise, find a place where you can reflect upon your life story. Think of the good and the bad, the happy and the sad, the times of abundance and the times of struggle. Select a journal, a notebook, a blog or even a voice recorder to capture your story. As you begin the process, go someplace that will inspire you to think clearly without disruptions.

As you think about your life, choose a time when you faced major decisions. This may be a time from your childhood or during recent years when you were challenged to either follow the crowd or live life differently. What did you choose, and what was it that made you want to rebel against the norm and take a risk into uncharted waters? Who influenced you the most and what life principles did you learn? As you recall the events, briefly describe how they impacted your thinking, challenged your assumptions, and/or clarified your values.

Your story may entail a spiritual component or it may not. The story you select should inspire thought and provide you with insight on where and how best to connect with others. Try to focus the section of your story into a single word that captures the heart. You may even want to create a slogan or motto that sums up your story. Remember, your story does not need to cover your entire life, nor does it need to entail every detail. What your story should do is provide you with a framework of your underlying thoughts, actions, and beliefs.

WHY PEOPLE GIVE?

> *I have found that among its other benefits,*
> *giving liberates the soul of the giver.*
> —Maya Angelou

In the business world, many people give to get. It is the name of the game. After attending what feels like hundreds of fundraising events, I tend to observe each event with a critical eye. Who does what better? Why is this event better or worse than the previous one? How is it unique to the demographics in which it is being held? As a philanthropic leader, I scrutinize fundraising events so that I can give quality feedback to organizations of what worked well or what could have been done differently. Likewise, I might share ideas about one charity event to another group so that they too may have a stronger fundraiser. Nevertheless, throughout the years I continue to see how many businesses and others will go to great extremes to look philanthropic only to attempt to gain a fast buck.

A while ago, my wife, Dixie, and I were invited to attend a $10,000 a plate dinner for a health charity in Palm Beach, Florida. All of our expenses would be paid, including hotel. When I learned of all of the details and realized that we would also get to connect with some dear friends, then I decided that it would be a fun event to attend.

Unbeknownst to me at the time, a corporation paid around $100,000 for a handful of individuals, including myself, to attend this particular fundraiser. They were there to make a generous donation on behalf of the charity, while attempting to close a business deal with each invited guest. After investigating this particular company for more than a year, my wife and I finally discovered that this particular group was not right for us.

What was fascinating about this particular company is that they wanted millions of dollars from a handful of individuals. And while they had major financial and legal problems of their own, they were willing to give around a hundred thousand dollars to look socially responsible and rich.

This group had major ethical, legal, and financial troubles brewing beneath the surface. On the surface, their philanthropic activity appeared generous, fun and good. The moral of this story is that many companies—

both good and bad—will throw lavish charitable events or donate large sums of money in order to generate more cash flow for themselves.

Many companies also give to charity because they truly want to be socially responsible in their community. In either case, people receive tax deductions, and thus, many give to get. Giving to receive more business, better public awareness, or whatever the offer is, continues to be a major reason so many individuals and corporations engage in the world of philanthropy.

PEOPLE GIVE TO SEE AND BE SEEN

People also give to increase their social and professional network. These individuals love being seen at the black-tie galas and they love having their picture taken at such events in hopes of making their local social column in their local magazines. Most people who fall under this category do not practice philanthropic leadership. Many of these individuals spend more money on their party wardrobes than on actually making a positive difference in the lives of others. They want to see and be seen.

A good number of these individuals are repeat donors and they make for a good party, but beyond the party, you should not expect that they will want to serve. This is not to totally discount their contribution, their awareness, and their presence, but it is simply to be honest about a particular group of donors. If you build a proper relationship with these individuals, you may eventually be able to influence some individuals to be more active than simply social.

PRIDE

Live auctions are great places for donors to bask in the spotlight of pride. At large fundraising events where the money can reach into the millions, often bidding philanthropists are moved more by their pride to out bid their friends, than they are about the actual cause. A competitive spirit of pride often drives up bids at auctions, and hopefully helps the cause of philanthropy.

Whether the auction benefits the arts or AIDS, pride motivates many people to become generous givers. Appealing to pride continues to be a major reason why individuals enter the arena of philanthropy. Some donors want their names forever engraved in buildings, so they donate out of pride. Or they like to throw lavish events to display their good works for all to see. Whatever the case may be, pride fuels these people's passion to give.

PAIN

Pain is another driver that fuels philanthropic action. Going through grief and painful experiences in life often produces positive philanthropic initiatives. When people experience need or personal pain, and once they come through those moments in life, they often desire to help others the way they were helped or would have liked to been helped. Whether it is a meals-on-wheels program like God's Love based in New York City, or simply helping a person through a tough time in their life, pain often produces acts of kindness to the benefit of others.

Susan G. Komen who took the lead in breast cancer awareness and research is one example. This national philanthropic initiative is a shining example of how pain can produce a major leading public charity. From missing children searches to Relay for Life, many great philanthropic charities are born out of a state of deep pain.

As a philanthropic leader, you may have some deep-rooted pain from your past that has sparked your interest in helping others. Your passion from personal pain may not be the next mega foundation, but that does not mean you should not consider your own past pain to promote philanthropy.

Several years ago, my wife was the executor of a widow's estate. This particular woman had no children, nor did she have any family nearby. Shortly after her death, my wife established a program in Orlando that originated in Oregon, *No One Dies Alone*. This charity is a volunteer based program where men and women sit with those who are dying in hospital beds. These individuals do not have family or friends or they do not have anyone who can get to them during their time of death. This program started because we saw our friend die and we wanted to be a presence in the lives of others going through similar circumstances. This is an example of philanthropy in action where giving is all about humans caring for one another. *No One Dies Alone* does not require money, just willing people who desire to share their love with strangers.

ACCOUNTANTS & TAX ATTORNEYS

You probably know by now you give when your accountants and tax attorneys advise you to give. Typically, these advisors do not care to whom your acts of charity benefit, or how involved you are in the process, they simply want you to transfer certain amounts of stocks, funds, and other assets at specific times during the year to minimize your taxes.

Many Americans qualify this type of giving as their social duty without actually immersing themselves in any more thought with those they give to. The common belief is "it is simply what must be done in order to do good business."

GUILT

Many people give large sums of money to different charities because of a deep seed of guilt. Maybe a loved one died and they believe they did not do enough to try to help, so now they give to health charities. Or maybe they were not there for their children, so now they serve in a youth mission like the Boy or Girl's Club. For whatever reasons, these individuals feel guilty for something they did or something they did not do, so now they find themselves in a place in their lives whereby they want to give back. They give back in hopes to ease or even erase their feelings of guilt.

A SERVANT'S HEART

Faith motivates many people to give. When you feel a deep spiritual call in your life to be a giver, you tend to give from your religious tradition. Mother Teresa rises to the top of the list when one thinks of a philanthropic leader with a servant's heart. It was her deep faith in God, her belief that philanthropy means loving another soul, and her ability to ignore the crowds, which allowed her to make a difference in the lives of so many in Calcutta, India. Her ongoing ability to serve, love, and give dignity to the death and dying came from her servant's heart. Many, like Mother Teresa, continue acts of giving from a position of humility rather than honor, poverty rather than power, and faith rather than fame.

It is the unsung heroes, the unknown servants of faith, and the anonymous givers who maintain the heart and soul of what it means to be a philanthropic leader. This may be you, your great grandmother, or someone in your neighborhood, who will never make the headlines like the Ted Turners and Bill Gates of the world, and they may never travel to far distant lands like India, but they give from the foundation of their faith like a servant who serves without being noticed.

Philanthropic leaders with servants' hearts understand that giving is not about them. And they understand that it is not about the temporal benefits: tax deductions, promotions, or corporate social responsibility. Rather, philanthropy is motivated by a deep love for their God, which compels them to be a blessing to others. They know that philanthropy means loving another person, even when it is not convenient, or the popular thing to do. Like a servant, they give up their rights to serve another person. In a nutshell, these philanthropic leaders who maintain servants' hearts care deeply and passionately about people. They realize that the most meaningful and significant acts of charity do not necessarily come from money, but love. You may find what a person needs more than money is financial wisdom, accountability, and direction in his or her life.

This is what being a philanthropic leader is all about. It is about loving another with humility, responsibility, and integrity. It entails empowering others with hope, dignity, and love. It is giving tools, wisdom, and encouragement to show the world that philanthropy is not so much about your checkbook, but ultimately about how your heart connects with another heart, how your life impacts the life of another soul for its well-being. Since the philanthropic life is a life of giving, you should desire to give from a pure heart with deliberate, good-intentioned results in mind.

LEADERSHIP EXERCISE: WHY DO YOU GIVE?

People give for many different reasons. Take time and reflect on why you give. You may have started your giving journey as a tax strategy for estate planning, but now you may want to give for greater reasons. Or you may have undergone a painful experience that fuels the fire in your giving. Whatever the reasons, it is important to clarify why you give. In this exercise, the following questions bring clarity to why you give.

1. Why do you really want to be a generous giver?
2. What hidden motives have fueled your giving in the past?
3. If you were to ask your friends or family why you like to engage in philanthropy, what would they most likely say? If you don't know, then ask them.
4. Have you ever given from a painful experience? If so, describe what you did and the pain that compelled you to give.
5. What religious or spiritual beliefs and values influence your giving habits?

WHERE HAVE YOU COME FROM?

All things must come to the soul from its roots, from where it is planted.
—Saint Teresa of Avila

Everyone comes from a spirit of selfishness. Young children do not have to be taught selfishness. Sharing is something that must be learned, practiced, and ultimately built into our Deoxyribonucleic acid (DNA), if we are ever to grow up and mature. Likewise, when it comes to philanthropy, most people really do not want to part with their money, time, or other resources.

Recently, I attended a Generous Giving Conference (www.generousgiving.org) where several individuals took the microphone to talk about the joys of giving. But when these individuals were really honest, the majority of them found it very hard to begin the discipline of giving. Some presenters could not figure out how they could give money on their current budget, still pay their bills and live with any comfort of knowing they had saved for a rainy day. Others knew how to generate great sums of wealth, and they were even great at preserving it, but they found it difficult to be a blessing to others by giving large sums of money to charity. After all, these wealthy individuals believed, "this is my money and I can use it however I like. Why should I give it to someone else who has not worked for it, or who does not truly value it like I do?"

In one sense, we all have come from the same place. Our nature is one of selfishness, and left unchecked selfishness leads to greed, idolatry, and many other grievous forms of fraud, manipulation, and arrogance. These crimes of selfishness are currently being manifested on Wall Street and across Main Street USA with our current economic meltdown.

It is easy to take note of the blind spots of selfishness in others, but how well do we see it in our own lives? The blind spots of selfishness, greed, and idolatry tend to reveal themselves where there is great excess and accumulation of wealth. And even when a bold friend or family member tells us that we should be more giving, that we have too much, or that we are too self-centered with our wealth, then we often brush these people off as if they are envious of what we have. Rather than taking a rebuke, checking our heart, or examining our true motives, our selfish nature tends to rise up in self-defense.

> ## LIFE PRINCIPLE: ONE OF THE BEST
> ## ANTIDOTES TO SELFISHNESS IS SHARING

Most of our parents taught us to share our toys when we were children. Some families practiced tithing to their local church, mosque, or synagogue. And the majority of us have participated in some form of charitable giving event at one point or another in our lives. However, if you find yourself struggling to be generous, or if you feel that giving money seems like a futile exercise, then now is the time to put away your selfish nature, and realize who you are when you give.

Knowing where you have come from determines what type of philanthropic leader you will become. Often those who have come from winning the battle of cancer will begin to lead philanthropically to fight against cancer. Those like Susan G. Komen to Lance Armstrong have led significant initiatives as a result of where they have come from. Others like Candy Lightner who over twenty-five years ago came from a place of great grief to start MADD (Mothers Against Drunk Driving).

Be it a place of pain or spiritual disciplines you learned as a child, your past reveals a story about why you believe what you believe today and why you do what you do. If you have not completed the leadership exercise about your story, now is the time to go back and do it. If you have completed the exercise, now is the time to reflect upon what you wrote. You may also want to reflect on your personal reasons for giving.

Your past offers jewels of insight into your future, if you take the time to reflect and look for them. For me personally, a family trip to Mexico when I was a child solidified my commitment to helping those in dire need. For the very first time, I saw other children my own age living in cardboard boxes with their parents on the filthy streets of Mexico. The images of those families remain forever burned into my heart and mind. As a result, I realize how blessed I have been all of my life, and I have made it a priority to be kind to the poor.

Other mission trips to the inner cities of America and to the sun scorched land of Africa have taken me through slums, open sewage and into Rwandan genocide sites. I have witnessed first hand some of the greatest devastation known to humanity.

Out of these past experiences, I process current needs, strategies, and philanthropic initiatives. Witnessing many of the terrible evils of our world shapes my perspective on current and future giving. This is not only true for me; it is also true for you. Becoming a philanthropic leader requires you to cultivate the discipline of reflecting on your past to determine how it influences your thoughts and beliefs. Going from one black-tie ball to another does not grip the heart and soul of the philanthropic leader. First hand experience of cancer, poverty, homelessness, or some other event in your life that forever changed you does. You may have never had cancer like Lance Armstrong, or you may have never had a child die from a drunk driver, but your personal life experiences, combined with a compassionate heart and kindness for others, can help many people.

After returning from a Guatemalan medical mission trip in the early 1990s, I looked around and could see so much needless spending here in America. Having gone without running water, fast food, and very limited electricity in Guatemala, I realized that I too could live on far less. And then, armed with new knowledge and wisdom, I began to survey all of the many mega churches and missions in America who claim they need millions upon millions of dollars in order to reach another person. I learned that many of these needs in America are simply conveniences.

The ability to scrutinize and interrogate true needs from mere conveniences may be one of your greatest challenges. When you combine where you have come from with personal experience of the lifestyles and needs of so many people in the world who live with so much less, you will be able to better weigh true needs, and do more with less.

LEADERSHIP EXERCISE

In today's exercise, what moments from your past continue to influence your thinking and beliefs as a philanthropic leader? Describe how those experiences have shaped and formed your thinking.

THE BURDENS OF GIVING

Money and time are the heaviest burdens of life, and the unhappiest of all mortals are those who have more of either than they know how to use.
—Samuel Johnson

Philanthropic leadership is rarely easy. The task at hand is not only challenging, it is emotionally taxing. As Aristotle said, "To give money away is an easy matter and in any man's power. But to decide to whom to give it, and how large and when, and for what purposes and how, is neither in every man's power nor an easy matter." His words continue to ring true today. When you survey the enormous needs at hand, and realize that all of the money in the world would not be enough, you begin to feel the burdens of giving.

Sometimes another request to give from a neighbor, friend, or executive director is simply too much. There will be times when you are tired of giving and it will feel like people only want you for your money. Not only will you feel that others only want you for your money, but you will also feel that many times these organizations do not understand how difficult it is for you to keep giving, year after year, as if nothing in your financial portfolio has changed. Never mind inflation, or that you have experienced a downturn in the stock market, or that you are simply not making the money you once did. All of those considerations do not really matter, because all that seems to matter to nonprofits is matching last year's contribution and perhaps giving more this year.

You do not want to disappoint those who are looking to you for support, but at the same time, there will be times in your philanthropic life when you are simply too tired to keep giving. You have given to the local charity year after year, and this year you simply want to step back and not give. But how do you not give without feeling like a failure? You have been reliable for many years, but now you are tired. If you have never felt burned out by giving, you will. If you have felt burned out by giving, then you understand those moments when you simply want to disappear. This is not the time to run and hide; it is time to go through the refining fires of giving.

BURNED BY CHARITY

If you have been in the business of giving for any amount of time, sooner or later charity will burn you. Several years ago, a handful of individuals gathered to form a new nonprofit organization. This public charity relied heavily on a couple of major donors. The organization was primarily built around one key individual to secure the future of his life's work. Problems began before anyone truly realized what had happened. One or two initial donors really needed and wanted a tax deduction, but their heart and soul were not in it.

After much debate, the group decided to establish a 501 (c) 3, rather than being investors in a for profit enterprise. This one decision, created primarily to cater to two individuals who only wanted a tax deduction and who never truly cared about the mission of the organization, ended up costing the organization dearly. The two donors should have simply given their money to another charity to receive a tax deduction. Nevertheless, this group has struggled for years to generate sufficient funding, and as a result the key individual, the 501 (c) 3 that was established to help, is no longer with the organization. He is now working in the business world. Other key donors felt betrayed, used, and abused by their generous donations.

BURNED BY THE MAILING LIST

As a generous giver, I am approached all of the time to not only give money, but also to bring my friends along. Organizations want my address book. This is nothing more than a strategic way of expanding their donor base. However, my wife and I have made it our policy to keep our friends as friends by not sharing their personal information.

When you play the tit-for-tat game (I gave to your cause, now you must give to my cause), the vicious cycle rarely ends. And when the cycle does end, for they eventually do, often it ends with people you once considered your generous friends as your enemies. The love is gone, and both friends and charities suffer. Ultimately, it is best to keep your friends as friends. But, if they want to connect with a particular charity, then simply connect them without having any strings attached.

Isn't that Earmarked?

A typical afternoon in my home office is spent looking at funding requests from organizations all over the world. Some are written well, and others are poorly written. One particular afternoon, my wife and I received a letter requesting us to pray and consider funding a particular project. This letter was intriguing; it offered a handful of different projects that needed funding. Each project needed the same amount of funding and each project was tastefully illustrated with pictures and a brief description.

After reading over each individual project, we decided to fund a particular project that was meaningful to where we were in our life. She wanted to fund half of the project, but with an urge to be overly generous, I wanted to fund the entire project. "If we are to be generous, let's go all out," I suggested. "We can afford the entire amount." Besides, we both felt a sentimental draw toward this specific project. We knew the enormous problem that this charity was attempting to address and we believed our contribution would create positive change. Ultimately, we chose to go ahead and fund the entire project for a sentimental reason.

> ## Life Principle: Be Quick to
> ## Listen and Slow to Give

About two and a half years later, the project we funded never had come to fruition. This of course sparked our concern. What we discovered was quite astonishing. Our donation actually went to fund another project and not the one we had chosen. This brought shock and awe, then a quick investigation. I asked our personal banker to pull the check that had been cleared two years ago and, as I thought, it was clearly earmarked in the memo section. Then I tried to pull documents and the original marketing letter that we had received, but it was nowhere to be found. After much prayer and thought and discussion with my wife, I proceeded to clarify any miscommunication. We wanted to know how our donation was misappropriated.

I learned that the original marketing material and grant request were misleading. The original letter appeared as if all the charity needed was money to execute the project. However, the project was never even ready to go to production. The initial funding request was not only misleading, but also deceitful.

When occurrences like this happen, and they will, you must decide how to clarify the confusion. One form of leadership will simply turn the cheek and walk away, another form will want to file a lawsuit and expose the organization. My wisdom born of experience is that neither choice is the best, although more and more public charities are being sued for misappropriating earmarked funds.

Typically, there is a third and fourth choice you can make as you navigate through choppy waters. It is best to have everything in writing and to ask the hard questions to determine what happened. We live in a fallen world, and mistakes will occur. Sometimes blatant deception arises. When giving large financial gifts, it is best to ask a lot of questions prior to giving, to investigate the integrity of the organization, and to ask to actively participate in the project. Even when you ask what you believe are simple questions, you may find avoidance in lieu of answers, and that an organization only wants your money. Beware if an organization does not desire your insight, wisdom, or perspective and only wants your cash. When you find yourself in such difficult circumstances, remember to use these moments for listening, learning, loving, and maturing as a philanthropic leader.

LET YOUR WORDS BE FEW

The richest man who ever lived, King Solomon, reminds us not to be too quick to promise anything.[2] Your words, as a philanthropic leader can come back to burn you if you are not careful. When you begin to be known as a philanthropic leader, then those seeking funding will begin to listen to what you have to say.

Excitement can override wisdom when you are approached to fund, sponsor, and/or participate in a new venture, a new ministry, or charity. Be careful not to allow the excitement of others to entrap you. Discerning between excitement and wisdom combined with knowledge is difficult when an emotional attachment is formed. As a philanthropic leader you

---

2 See Ecclesiastes 5:2.

must learn to make decisions based on wisdom, knowledge and the beliefs you hold, not purely on emotional responses. This is easier said than done, but it is best to be slow to speak as you develop a holistic approach to your leadership.

DECEPTION, LIES AND VOICE MESSAGES

One evening, my wife and I had just returned home from a long trip when we decided to check our voice messages. We immediately recognized the voice that came through the machine. It was an executive director of a nonprofit Christian ministry. He spoke with great enthusiasm about how wonderful everything was going for the ministry. His excitement and positivism came roaring through our phone line as we listened, and then he said, "Goodbye." He thought the line was dead. Little did he know, what he was about to say to another employee of the organization would also be recorded on our machine for us to hear.

At this point, he truly had our attention. He began to share a completely different story and perspective to the employee who was with him. What we heard was shocking and deceptive. The executive director said to the other employee, "We will just fold the ministry and they will forgive the loan. Then we can create a new entity with our current assets, yet we will not have any debt." The captured conversation went on a little more, but, for the most part, this story line was radically different from the positive one intentionally left on our machine. Experiences like this will cause you not to ever want to trust another person, no matter how nice they may appear or how worthy of a cause they work for.

SO MANY OPTIONS

There are so many options when it comes to practicing philanthropic leadership. When you are not clear about your values and beliefs, and when you do not have a clear vision of what you want to accomplish in relationship with others, then the options will be overwhelming. The more overwhelmed you feel, especially during the holiday season when grant requests are at the highest of the year, the more difficult it is to maneuver through all of the letters. With so much need, and so little clarity, giving a little bit to everyone who asks usually does not make a significant difference. Yet, saying no to so many requests often brings feelings of guilt and shame. When you get pulled into this cycle, the stress of deciding who to give to, how much to give, and when, seem to push many philanthropists over the edge to a place where they become numb. And even though all of the requests are not for your money, the majority of them are. Nevertheless, some requests will want you to volunteer your time in a soup kitchen, children's home, or some other endeavor.

NUMB: GIMME SOME MORE

In the last decade, the mega, global rock star and philanthropic leader, Bono sings "Gimme some more, gimme some more, gimme some more, too much is not enough. Gimme some more, gimme some more, gimme some more, too much is not enough ..."[4] The name of the song in the remix version is *Numb*. Too often, donors feel like all nonprofits want is just a little bit more and, as a result, the philanthropic leader becomes numb to giving. This feeling tends to come after experiencing the burdens of giving. Since you do not have unlimited financial resources, you will never be able to give to every person who asks nor will you be able to give the amount of money that they want. When you begin to feel numb toward giving, your giving days are not over, but they may simply be on pause.

Taking a pause from being generous is a good thing. We all need time to rest, renew, and reflect on what is truly important in life. Taking sabbaticals from being charitable does not mean you are no longer a philanthropic leader. On the contrary, it simply gives you the opportunity to regain strength, focus, and clarity on what has worked well in your leadership and what has not. By taking a break from giving, you will find the needed rest to renew your heart, thoughts, and emotions from having gone through the burdens of giving.

The burdens do not necessarily go away, but by going through them again and again, you will be better able to manage the ugly side of giving with more grace, better leadership, and experience. It is here where your strategies of giving, your expectations, and your leadership should improve by being refined by the fire, rather than by being burned. Be honest about how you feel when you are in the refining fires of giving. Let other organizations know that you are simply on pause this year or month and that after taking a better inventory of your current philanthropic plan, you will get back with them and let them know what you will or will not do. It is also beneficial to take note of how organizations respond to you during moments where you simply feel overwhelmed in your giving. Do they respect your current feelings or do they continue to press you for more? As Dr. Paul Schervish, the Director of the Center on Wealth and Philanthropy at Boston College asks, "Do these people ask you to give or do they tell you to give?"[5] Is it a request or a demand?

LEADERSHIP EXERCISE

1. Describe how you process the burdens of giving.

2. Has there ever been a time when you felt people only wanted your money? How did that make you feel? What did you do?

3. What policies and procedures do you need to implement to protect you from burnout?

4. Do you have a group of friends, advisors, or confidants with whom you can share the burdens of giving? If not, then make a list of three to five trustworthy people who understand the burdens of giving. Start a conversation with these individuals about these burdens.

5. If you were going to take a sabbatical from giving, what would it look like? How much time do you need? And what specific goals would you like to achieve during this time of rest, renewal, and reflection?

THE BLESSINGS OF GIVING

For it is in giving that we receive.
—Saint Francis of Assisi

The blessings of giving are internal and external, temporal and eternal. They are both tangible and intangible. Blessings come in all kinds of shapes and sizes from a smile to a hug, to tears of joy and happiness. It is through giving where human lives transcend their own agendas to connect with another person. The mere fact that people desire to help each other is a blessing unto life and relationships. But the blessing of giving is truly worth rejoicing when recipients of charity transform into generous givers themselves. By building the right character into the life of another person where he or she becomes a blessing to others is the ultimate goal from generation to generation.

SURPRISED! AN UNEXPECTED GIFT

Sometimes in your journey as a philanthropic leader, you will feel the deep urge simply to surprise another person with an unexpected gift of love. This type of behavior should not be your typical strategy for giving, but as a giver, you should be open to the idea that sometimes, without explanation, you simply want to bless another person. This is one of my most favorite forms of blessing another life. Let me share with you several examples of giving a surprise.

UNITED PARCEL SERVICE (UPS) & THE GARBAGE COLLECTOR

One Christmas, I surprised a handful of people with an unexpected gift. I gave small amounts of cash to those who serve me all year long. From the garbage collector to our UPS deliveryman, I wanted to bless these individuals. This concept is nothing new, and is practiced by many philanthropic leaders yearly during the holidays. I have given everything from cigars to electricians to taking different service individuals to play a round of golf. If you feel really comfortable with all the many different people who add value in your life, then you should discover ways to surprise them. It is about what they would find good and desirous rather than what you would.

A CARD WITH CASH

One Christmas afternoon, the toys had been opened and the single-parent mother finally sat in her home all alone. Her son was now with dad, and she was turning to her stack of Christmas cards. Not expecting anything but a nice note, she turned to the card that my wife and I had sent her. After reading it, the tears of joy, gratitude, and blessing burst forth. We gave her a check for $10,000 to use however she saw fit. It was not so much the amount, but the act of giving that counted, for this woman became utterly speechless. She was blown away by our generosity, and we too were moved to tears of joy that we could hopefully make a small difference in her life. We have given many gifts like this over the years to family members, friends, past employees, and others whom we feel a deep urge to surprise. But we always make it clear to the individual recipients that this is a one-time gift, and not to be expected again. My wife and I usually convey to the recipient that he or she has been a blessing in our life, and for them to receive the check not so much from our hand but from the hand of God.

HAPPY MEALS & McDONALDS

I had the privilege of speaking on behalf of an international human rights organization to a church in Orlando, Florida. This particular church was highlighting an international mission and a local mission each Sunday over that particular summer. I was there to speak on behalf of the international mission, and another gentleman was there to speak on behalf of a local children's home. In this particular instance the gentleman speaking on behalf of the home had sixteen of the children there present to sing a song for the congregation. After hearing the children sing and listening to the executive director's need for the home, my heart was compelled to get involved. And when you are compelled to give, you take action.

As soon as the service was over, I asked the executive director of the children's home what his and the children's plans were immediately after the meet-and-greet session. I suggested that I would love the opportunity to take the children to lunch at McDonalds. "What? You want to take all of us out to eat? You've got to be kidding? Yes, you can buy all of these kids lunch today if you really want!" Then came the next set of questions. "Who are you? What do you do? Are you sure? I did hear your presentation on the international human rights organization, now do you work for them?" I responded, "I want to be a friend, get to know you and the children, and be a blessing. I'll see you at McDonalds."

My relationship with the children's home started over Happy Meals. It was a joy seeing all of these kids' eyes light up, knowing that they could order anything they wanted and as much as they wanted at McDonalds. Afterwards, they all gave me a hug, a handshake, or other kind of "thank you," which brought tears of blessing to my eyes. As a result, I continue to work with this organization to this day.

PROFESSIONAL ATHLETES

Throughout the years you have probably watched commercials on television showing National Football League (NFL) players and the United Way, a professional golfer making the difference in the life of a child, or some other professional athlete taking time to visit the sick, adopt a highway clean up project, or donate all of his or her cash earnings to charity. The Dallas Morning News reported on November 20, 2008, Tony Romo, quarterback for the Dallas Cowboys extended acts of love and kindness to a homeless man by sharing a day at the movies. This type of charity and act of kindness is both easy and a blessing. It is giving to another without expecting anything in return. It allows both the giver and the receiver to be blessed.

A few years back, neighbors of mine, Justin and Kate Rose, did just this to the same children's home that I have had the privilege of working with (as mentioned above). Justine Rose had won a $100,000 check to donate through the annual Tavistock Golf Tournament. He and his wife were simply driving down the road, saw the children's home, and thought the home would be a good group to donate his earnings to. What a surprise and unexpected gift! This not only gave the children's home a sizeable economic gift, but also it gave them much needed publicity and a new relationship. Since the initial sizeable donation, the Rose family has been able to donate other professional golf memorabilia for the home to auction off at their annual fundraiser.

When gifts like this become public and when they are given by a public figure, like a professional golfer, this often spurs other wealthy philanthropists to get involved with the same organization. The logic often goes like this: "If Justin Rose thinks this charity is worthy of his time and money and endorsement, then maybe I should look into it as well." And when this occurs, momentum builds, and others step up, often with matching gifts. Nevertheless, if you have public name power, then you need to understand how you can be a blessing by endorsing a cause or charity.

A Delayed Response

Five years ago, my wife and I attended a fundraising banquet for International Justice Mission (IJM) (www.ijm.org). We sat in the back of a large ballroom, ate the typical rubber chicken, while listening to Gary Haugen, the founder and President of IJM speak. He spoke about the mission, work, and the need for IJM. Toward the end of the program, the organization offered guests time to make a financial donation to their organization. My wife and I got up and slowly left the building. We have heard what feels like hundreds upon hundreds of giving requests at such events; we were not in the mood to sit through another one. On the way home, Dixie and I discussed IJM. We both liked what we had heard, but we did not feel that this was the time or that the banquet was the place to get involved. Months later, International Justice Mission came to mind as we read *Redeeming Love*, a fiction book on prostitution and oppression. Moved by the book, moved by what we had heard several months prior, and moved by God, we decided that we wanted to actively begin a relationship with IJM. We decided to make a sizeable donation on behalf of widows, orphans, and the sexually oppressed around the world through the work of IJM. So, I picked up the phone one day, called IJM and said we wanted to be a blessing. Hearing the amount that we wanted to donate, the woman on the other end of the phone asked whom I had been working with within their organization. I knew that she assumed that a person on their development team had been in close contact with me. When I quickly responded that no one had been in contact with me, it made the blessing all the more surprising for IJM. Sometimes the best surprises may feel delayed, but the recipients tend to convey that the blessings were never late.

These stories represent many different ways you can be a blessing to others as a giver. There are countless other blessings that come from giving: inner peace, joy, and excitement to name a few. It often seems like the more generous you are, the more blessed you become.

AN INSTANT RESPONSE

About a month after the earthquake killed so many lives in Port-au-Prince Haiti, I had the privilege of serving Danita's Children, a children's center for orphans in Ouanaminthe, Haiti. Serving alongside 17 other volunteers from the States, we discovered that the organization needed a generator for their boy's home. As a result, the 17 volunteers, including myself, were able to pull our cash on-hand together, and the next day a couple of us took a drive to Cap-Haitien, Haiti to purchase a generator and personally take it back to Danita's Children in the back of a pick-up truck. This type of instant response to a philanthropic need is another way you can bless a charity. Those who gave saw a need, and personally took responsibility to meet the need. We did not wait until we got back to the States to raise money, or purchase a generator here and then ship it to Haiti. But on the contrary, we made it happen instantly.

LEADERSHIP EXERCISE: BE A BLESSING

In this exercise, your challenge is to be a blessing to others. By creating strategic opportunities to bless other people, take the initiative to surprise others through your philanthropic leadership. This exercise requires you to bless a different person each month for an entire year. Be creative in your giving and think of creative ways you can be a blessing to another person.

1. Make a list of twelve people you can be a blessing to this year. Choose twelve people whom you have never blessed in a meaningful and significant way. Make each blessing an opportunity to connect with them in a way that honors them and makes them feel special. Know why you want to bless each person you have chosen over the next twelve months. Then decide when and where and how you will be a blessing to them.

2. Keep a journal and each time you bless someone from your list write what you learned from the experience. Whose life did you impact? Why did you choose them? How did you make a difference in their life? What did you learn from the experience about yourself? What did you learn from the experience about them? What would you have done differently? What would you keep the same?

Your Calling

Every person has a certain mission that they are called to fulfill.
—Johann Wolfgang von Goethe

Being a philanthropic leader is not about holding a certain position or having a specific job title. The world has too many job titles and position holders who look like they are making a difference in the lives of others. If showing up at black-tie galas, participating in community ribbon cuttings, and wining and dining the upper echelon in your society is what you believe philanthropic leadership is, then think again. Philanthropic leadership is not simply being a high net worth donor or contributing to your local charities. Philanthropic leadership is a way of living. It is not something you simply do out of your private foundation or when your accountant and tax attorney instruct you to make some capital gains contributions; instead, it is a new way of thinking about charity, money and leadership. Philanthropic leadership is less concerned about counting receipts, and more concerned about empowering the widow and orphan to live a life where they become philanthropic leaders within their own circle of influence.

The philanthropic leader is sick and tired of receiving funding requests month after month from charitable organizations, which believe money is the answer to the world's greatest problems. The philanthropic leader is one who realizes that the organization that does not know how to properly manage the resources it is freely given should not continue to freely receive. Accountability comes with a price. The philanthropic leader believes that the quantity of a gift is less important than the quality of the person giving it. In the days of Jesus, He said that a poor widow put more money into the Temple's offering than the rich who simply gave out of their wealth; this example illustrates that being a giver is not so much about how much you give, but about the heart behind your giving. It is not how much money you have, if you volunteer at the local soup kitchen, or if you desire to make lots of money so that you can give it away. No, philanthropic leadership is all about the heart. When your heart says as Martin Luther's once did, "Here I stand, I can do no other," then you are about to respond to the heart call of what it means to become a philanthropic leader.

LIFE PRINCIPLE: YOUR CALLING
ENRAPTURES YOUR SOUL

Philanthropic leadership begins with a calling. Webster's dictionary defines this feeling, this call, as "a strong inner impulse toward a particular course of action especially when accompanied by conviction of divine influence." In other words, the calling originates from a relationship to help others. And since the call is based on a relationship rather than on money, the philanthropic leader understands that a greater purpose exists above and beyond the transaction of giving. People matter. Lives count. And how the leader engages others does make a difference. If you believe your wealth gives you a position of superiority, then you truly do not understand the privilege and responsibility of the call to the philanthropic way of life. For the goal is not the accumulation of wealth, or even the distribution of it, but the goal is to radically answer the call to lead with courage, to love with hope, and to liberate with dignity.

The philanthropic way of life is one where the leader is set apart to serve others. This calling comes from a heart call of humility. It is not pride, power, or your position that qualifies you as a philanthropic leader. Pride, power, and the prestige of giving corrupt the work, the leadership, and the intentions behind philanthropy. Even though generosity is a virtue, there is great temptation in the hands of the one who calls the shots. As Duane Elmer eloquently writes:

> Simply put, giving is power. It is power to control valuable resources. It is power to select who is to receive and who will not receive. Therefore, it is power over people. This power can make giving a source of liberty and empowerment of another; or giving can further consolidate power in the giver, bringing inevitable isolation from other believers.[6]

The call of the philanthropic leader is not to use this power over people for self-promotion. It is a call to a serving, humble relationship for the greater good of the many. And it is in this calling where the relationship reflects a genuine receptivity of the thoughts, ideas, hopes, and dreams of others. It is a call to participate along with those you serve. As in the words from the Prophet Isaiah, "Is it not to share your food with the hungry, and to provide the poor wanderer with shelter; when you see the naked, to clothe him; and not to turn away from your own flesh and blood?"[3] Since the etymology of philanthropy is the "love of mankind," then your call as a philanthropic leader is to love others in such a way that you make a significant and transformational difference in their lives. The call is not to simply serve others for the sake of serving, but to transform them into servant leaders as well.

This type of loving another person fits with the tools and strategies of servant leadership coined from Robert Greenleaf. Servant leadership entails ten essential tools every philanthropic leader should develop: *listening, empathy, healing, awareness, persuasion, conceptualization, foresight, stewardship, commitment to the growth of people,* and *building community.*[7] These qualities come from a heart bent on serving others for their benefit. As you read through the list, ask yourself if you naturally possess these qualities, or if they are values you aspire to posses.

The following describes each quality:

1. Listening: Leaders have traditionally been valued for their communication and decision-making skills. While these are also important skills for the servant-leader, they need to be reinforced by a deep commitment to listening intently to others. He or she seeks to listen receptively to what is being said. Listening, coupled with regular periods of reflection, is essential to the growth of the servant-leader.

2. Empathy: The servant-leader strives to understand and empathize with others.

3. Healing: One of the greatest strengths of servant-leadership is the potential for healing one's self and others. Many people have broken spirits and have suffered from a variety of emotional hurt. Although this is part of being human, servant-leaders recognize that they also have an opportunity to "help make whole" those with whom they come in contact.

4. Awareness: General awareness, and especially self-awareness, strengthens the servant-leader. Awareness also aids one in understanding issues involving ethics and values. It lends itself to

---

3 Isaiah 58:7, *New International Version.*

being able to view most situations from a more integrated, holistic position.

5. Persuasion: Another characteristic of servant-leaders is a primary reliance on persuasion rather than positional authority in making decisions within an organization. The servant-leader seeks to convince others rather than coerce compliance.

6. Conceptualization: Servant-leaders seek to nurture their abilities to "dream great dreams."

7. Foresight: Foresight is a characteristic that enables the servant-leader to understand the lessons from the past, the realities of the present, and the likely consequences of a decision for the future.

8. Stewardship: Robert Greenleaf's view of all institutions was one in which CEOs, staffs, and trustees all played significant roles in holding their institutions in trust for the greater good of society. Servant-leadership, like stewardship, assumes first and foremost a commitment to serving the needs of others.

9. Commitment to the growth of people: Servant-leaders believe that people have an intrinsic value beyond their tangible contributions as workers.

10. Building Community: The servant-leader seeks to identify some means for building community among those who work within a given institution.[8]

Finally, your calling is a call to action. When you feel called to give, you cannot ignore the call. Your action is brought about from *listening* to the needs around you. Displaying a heart of *empathy* toward your fellow neighbor seems to draw you to want to bring *healing* and help to those closest to you. By engaging others at the heart level, you become *aware* of their needs and you desire to fulfill those needs. By practicing the art of *persuasion*, you do not use persuasion to advance your own agenda, but you use it to empower others by *conceptualizing* the great things that can be accomplished in a relationship. Through *strategic foresight* and responsible *stewardship*, your actions reveal your *commitment* to the growth of others in healthy ways, which *builds up* the *community* from which you serve. This is your calling. This is the way of living out that call with responsible action.

Leadership Exercise

1. Take your leadership journal and describe what it means to you as one called into philanthropy. Personalize your calling in such a way that you can clearly and concisely communicate it to others.

2. Do you believe "giving is power"? Describe how you might redirect your power to empower those you seek to serve.

3. Describe how you give from a heart of empathy.

4. How might you implement the ten character traits of servant leadership into your philanthropic leadership?

5. Why do you believe you are called to become a philanthropic leader?

CHAPTER TWO:
YOUR CORE VALUES AND BELIEFS

*You can't walk alone. Many have given the illusion, but none
have really walked alone. Man is not made that way. Each man is
bedded in his people, their history, their culture, and their values.*
—Peter Abrahams

YOUR CORE VALUES AND BELIEFS comprise the most important aspect of your leadership because they define who you are as a leader. Without a set of clearly defined values, your leadership compass will compel you in numerous directions. Some of the gravitational pulls you will face may be good, while others may lead you into dangerous waters of philanthropy. Everyone will want your money, time and attention. When you are not clear about your core values and beliefs, frustration and ultimately fatigue will arrive. You will feel used and abused. But when you have a clear understanding of your beliefs and your personal identity as a philanthropic leader, you feel energized to make a significant difference as you lead in alignment.

WHAT YOU BELIEVE MATTERS

What distinguishes the majority of men from the few is their inability to act according to their beliefs.
—John Stuart Mill

What you believe matters as a person, as a leader, and as a philanthropist. It matters if you believe you can make a difference in the world. It matters what you think about money, time, giving, and life. It matters what you believe about yourself as well as what you believe about other people. It matters what you believe about the rich and the poor. It matters what you believe the role government takes in relation to solving philanthropic social problems. It matters what you believe the local church, synagogue, and mosque's role is as well, and if you believe these religious groups can work together to make a difference. Beliefs matter.

If you believe that giving more money is the answer to some of the world's greatest problems, then this belief will impact your strategy and giving outlook. If you believe pouring more money at a problem may not be the best answer, then this will give you a completely different strategy. Not long ago I received a letter stating a particular belief: "money is muscle for ministry." This belief, that money is muscle for ministry, shapes and informs what this particular pastor believes about both money and ministry. This belief of course came with a dire plea for more money to be sent to his ministry. This particular belief is too common among religious leaders who tend to look to the almighty dollar rather than God. What you believe determines the type of philanthropic leader you will become.

LIFE PRINCIPLE: YOUR BELIEFS GUIDE YOUR THINKING

It is one thing to believe you can raise money, build a new building, or give all you have to the poor; it is quite another thing to believe the world does not need to raise any more money, build another building, or give all they have to the poor. The nonprofit organization, GiveWell, believes you should give less but accomplish more, as their website states (www.givewell.net). They "don't believe all charities are doing great work.

We don't even believe most of them are."⁹ GiveWell evaluates charities, foundations and other nonprofit organizations to know exactly who is making a real difference. Similarly, Calvin Edwards & Company (www.calvinedwardscompany.com) investigates charities for individual philanthropic leaders and private foundations to give objective counsel. Groups like these analyze charities to provide solid, sound advice to philanthropic leaders. By testing your assumptions and beliefs, measuring outcomes with goals, and observing the behavior of yourself and others, what you believe will eventually become very clear.

WHAT IS A BELIEF?

A belief is not a thought or ideal you loosely hold. It is not a mere hope you wish for. A belief is a core part of who you are. It is something you hold dearly, and may even fight for. Your beliefs guide your thinking. As you are well aware, I do not believe money is the answer to the world's greatest philanthropic needs. Rather, I strongly believe leaders need to engage followers in a loving relationship that creates independence rather than dependence. I believe that the majority of donors in America give only money, and that is wasteful. I believe too many nonprofits spend your money on their personal conveniences rather than on true needs. I believe your charity, foundation, and personal life will be healthier if you can live without debt. I believe just because I can give money away does not mean that I should. And I believe that most nonprofits should be for-profit companies who rise or fall by their ability to generate true sustainability by meeting real needs.

Although you may or may not agree with my beliefs, one thing is clear, when I know what I believe; *you know where I stand.* Knowing where you and others stand in regard to beliefs is vital for maintaining healthy relationships. If one person on your board or foundation believes raising more money is the answer to your problems and if you believe having better oversight and effective implementation is better, then your clash of beliefs may eventually cause problems. However, when everyone on your team participates together in open, transparent ways, then knowing what each member believes and working through those beliefs helps generate more effective team participation within your organization and/or giving strategy.

Your Worldview

When your beliefs and assumptions come together they form your worldview. A worldview consists of your answers to life's biggest questions regarding everything from God, people, poverty, ethics, and giving. Since the field of philanthropy attempts to bring real solutions to many of these major questions, you need to understand the role of a worldview. The role of a worldview informs your thinking about basic beliefs and assumptions. The type of worldview you hold determines how you form your beliefs. For example, where you stand on radical relativism or fundamental modernism influences your basic beliefs about ethics, human life and God. Because there are so many worldviews from relativism, modernism, post-modernism to the emerging worldviews of spirituality, your leadership strategies and thinking will either stand the test of time or they will fade away as latest trend emerges.

A worldview worth practicing should pass the test of reason, the test of experience in the real world, the test of your inner common sense, and the test of practice.[10] The test of reason entails the law of non-contradiction, which states, "A, which can stand for anything, cannot be both B and non-B at the same time in the same sense."[11] To illustrate, if a donor allocates a specific amount of money for a particular project, then the money must be used for such a project. If it is not, then the charity is in jeopardy of operating in an immoral and unethical way. Thus, your worldview should be logically sound.

Second, your worldview should correlate to what you perceive in the real world.[12] If you truly care about the poor, then your actions should reveal your beliefs. This not only brings alignment, but also it authenticates your beliefs. Then, "worldviews also need to fit what we know about ourselves. Examples of this kind of information include the following: I am a being who thinks, hopes, experiences pleasures and pain, beliefs, and desires."[13] This test is important because it provides you with the empathy needed to connect with those you serve. If you truly do not care about a particular cause, then you should not participate in a way that would lead others to believe that you do. Here again, the beliefs held within your worldview should align with who you are as a person.

Finally, the test of practice reveals whether or not your worldview holds up to the real world.[14] Believing that bed nets will prevent the spread of malaria in Africa and actually realizing that those nets tend to be used for everything *but* the prevention of malaria is a test of practice. This is why analyzing and reflecting upon philanthropic initiatives is so important for the progress of philanthropy.

As you mature in philanthropic leadership, it is vital to understand how you form your beliefs and the type of worldview you implement. This helps you understand who you are as a philanthropic leader, and it helps you relate to those you lead. Only leaders who confidently know what they believe in and why they believe the way they do are capable of withstanding the fires of philanthropy.

LEADERSHIP EXERCISE

1. Make a list of your top ten empowering beliefs as it relates to your views on being a philanthropic leader.
2. Make a list of beliefs you want to challenge, test, and possibly change. Create your own strategy to test and challenge these beliefs. Your strategy may simply entail a healthy debate with friends, or it may entail you to put your philanthropic leadership to practice. Either way, give yourself a deadline to complete the challenge and test, and then see if your beliefs have changed.
3. Make a list of what you believe about the poor, the rich, and giving.
4. Make a list of what you believe the purpose of life is all about.
5. Make a list of what commitments you believe are worth living out.

WHO ARE YOU?

We are what we believe we are.
—C. S. Lewis

Within the world of philanthropy, many donors, advocates, and volunteers work to promote their causes because their causes are an extension of who they are. Al Weiss, president of Walt Disney World Resorts is pouring his time, money, and effort into Vision 360, a church planting training facility, as a philanthropic leader. Why would a man who is busy leading Disney's many theme parks throughout the world spend his extra time, money, and energy into such a project? In order to understand the whys behind "why philanthropic leaders do what they do," you must know who they are.

Al Weiss lives authentically to his core beliefs, values, and passions. From one perspective he is a highly esteemed global business leader. Yet from another perspective he is the son of a church planting Baptist pastor. His childhood roots continue to inform and shape his philanthropic activity in adulthood. By combining his business leadership acumen along with his heart for training and helping the next generation of Christian pastors succeed, Weiss is a great example of not only what it means to be a philanthropic leader, but a man who lives accordingly to who he is.

As a result of his business experience and knowledge, Weiss understands the constant need of generating cash flow. His philanthropic leadership has established Vision 360 to be economically self-sufficient as it starts new churches all over the world. He fulfills his calling of spreading the Christian gospel in a way that is effective, efficient and financially sustainable by using his business wisdom. Weiss knows himself. He can do what he loves and, at the same time, continue to lead and preside over Disney. For Weiss, it is not simply an either/or decision—either I work at Disney or I engage in my religious beliefs as a philanthropist, but rather it is a both/and decision. This perspective allows Weiss to lead from a holistic, balanced life approach. He does not have to give up one for the other. He does both in a way that is energizing by living authentically from all of his passions and desires.

My trip to Mexico as a child and other similar adventures play a major part of my philanthropic work today. From a summer spent in the inner city of Chicago, feeding the homeless, playing with children, and visiting patients dying with HIV/AIDS to participating alongside surgeons in the developing world as a teenager, I have had opportunities to get in on the action. Seeing a baby born via a C-section in the developing world, bandaging the wounds of the sick and caring for the poor and hurting has challenged and shaped my beliefs about myself as well as others.

Going through different life experiences continues to mold your character, challenges your beliefs and shapes your thoughts about your place in the world. By reflecting upon your life, how have you developed as a person to bring you where you are today? What have been some of the most life-altering experiences that you've gone through? What makes you unique as a person, leader, and philanthropist?

In order for your leadership and life to be genuine, you must know who you truly are as a person. You live your beliefs in your daily life. You actively practice what you preach. Deep down in your heart and soul you know who you are, what you desire to be a part of, and what you dislike. There is profound simplicity from living an authentic life. Living from your desires, beliefs, and values brings clarity to the decisions you face, the leadership you practice, and places you invest your time. If you have found yourself participating in charities that are good, but not quite you, then now is the time to say no to those things that do not seem to ring true to your heart and say yes to those that do. You will begin to experience true freedom and joy as a philanthropic leader by investing in what you passionately believe in.

The passions of your life may have roots going back to your childhood or they may be new adventurous roads leading into your future. The important point is that you will invest your time, money, thoughts, and energy on where your passion is. When you are all alone and daydreaming, what thoughts keep you occupied? What difference do you want to make in the world and how? Who do you naturally gravitate to? And where do you naturally go in your thoughts and daily conversations? When you are on autopilot, who are you?

Although questions like these are important to wrestle with, it is also critical that you define who you are and what you are about. Followers want to follow leaders who lead from their passions and core identity rather than from the shifting winds of life. It is also important to understand your history of values, beliefs, and experiences to know how your past impacts your present and future.

As you clarify who you are, both the story you tell and the one you live, speak to your character. It is important to tell your story as you connect with others along the philanthropic journey of life. It is important to have your story crafted in such a way that your values, beliefs, and worldview emerge to reach beyond a job title, relationship status, or your economic status to the heart of another person.

One of the reasons I started this book with my story is because it is important to know who you are, where you have come from, and what makes you who you are. Stories captivate the heart, and they connect us to another person. Likewise, defining who you are is a powerful exercise in forming and shaping your philanthropic leadership. You most likely are generous and you want to excel in your leadership of generosity. The people you work with and serve alongside will want to know you and your heart. It is not enough to simply want to give money or help the needy. Just because Bill Gates may have generated more money than any living person in modern history, why has he really committed the latter part of his life to being a philanthropic leader? Many wealthy men and women before him did not choose a life of giving. Hence, it is important to realize the stories within the heart that drive individuals to lead and care for those they serve. For it is your story, it is how you see yourself in the world, what you think of others and money that will ultimately empower you to fulfill your calling as a philanthropic leader.

LEADERSHIP EXERCISE

Sharing your story and your life with others, as a philanthropic leader, is one of the greatest gifts you will ever give to another person. We all have stories to share with others. And when you enter into relationship with other people, your story helps bridge the hearts and souls of the relationship. Your story also gives encouragement and hope to the next generation, for often it is in your story where you and others discover who you truly are.

1. What are the critical milestones in your life that you find important to who you are?
2. What are the major four or five most important events or experiences in your life? How have these events impacted you?
3. What childhood experiences have you had that have fueled your desire to make a difference in the world?
4. What does your heart truly ache for that you have not had the opportunity to put into words or action?
5. Who has influenced your thinking about life, money, and giving? How have they influenced you?

Your Values

> *Love is the expression of one's values, the greatest reward*
> *you can earn for the moral qualities you have achieved in*
> *your character and person, the emotional price paid by one*
> *man for the joy he receives from the virtues of another.*
> —Ayn Rand

Just as every charity, foundation, and organization maintains both shared and unique values, so do you. You have values that are common to many other philanthropic leaders, people in your community, and the world at large, but you also maintain specific values that are unique to you. When you are able to hold both your common values and the values that set you apart from others in a proper balance and perspective, then your leadership will begin to reflect these values. Your values reveal your core identity of who you are when people are watching and when people are not. In order to live and lead in authentic relationships with others, your values must align with your actions. This of course is easier said than done but with consistent daily practice, you will begin to live with the natural power and energy that comes as a result of living in alignment with your values.

There are many types of values, things you may hold dearly to your heart and even lose your life over, but ultimately values fall into two different categories: you either have certain values, or you aspire to live up to certain values. There are the values you strive toward, and there are the values that you currently live by. One set of values is aspirational, while the other set is internal to who you are as a person. For example, if your character reveals to others that you not only value loyalty but that your life and leadership reflects loyalty in your daily habits, then you will be known as being a loyal person. However, you may value a mentoring relationship, yet not be in one. Here, you aspire to live in a mentoring relationship where you can begin to exercise this value as a leader. First, you need to clarify your aspirational values and the values that are true to your character.

> ## LIFE PRINCIPLE: YOUR VALUES MAY
> ## CHANGE IN AN INSTANT

There are also values in your life that may change over time or that you need to intentionally change. Undergoing a transformation of values sometimes occurs slowly and over many years, and other times this transformation occurs in an instant. For example, all it took was one car wreck killing Candy Lightner's daughter to create what would become known as Mothers Against Drunk Driving (MADD). In an instant, your life may be forever changed and with it, your values. Or your values may slowly transform over many years of growing, learning, and living. Life has a way of challenging your values. One day you may find yourself being abundantly generous, while years earlier your only thoughts where on how to make a lot of money. From a life of greed to a life of generosity, you may find your values have changed over the years.

Sometimes, your values will never change. These are your rock values. They do not shift with the seasons of life, and they do not seem to break no matter what kind of external pressure is forced upon them. No matter what storms of life come, these values remain solid as a rock. These values have carried you through the darkest days of your life and they will carry you through tough times ahead. These values give you the surety that you can weather the storm, you can keep going, and you can truly make a difference when all else doubt you. These values may come from your religious heritage, your family upbringing, or they are simply firm commitments that have been with you all your life. These are the values that feel as if they are a part of your DNA—they're hardwired. You cannot shake them, nor do you want to.

Then there are the diamond values. These too are as hard and unshakable as your rock values, but these values know how to bring out the sparkle not only in your life but also in the life of others. Your greatest diamond value may be summed in your covenantal vows of love you took at your wedding. The value of love brings sparkle and light to your life and to those closest to you. Many people benefit from this value. Or your diamond value may come when you hold an orphan in your arms; you bring a smile and a sparkle to the eyes of others.

The sparkle of these diamond values may come as the result of a man in the bush of Guatemala being able to smile for the very first time, realizing he can now go out and find a wife after receiving a cleft lip and palate surgery from a group like Smile Train or Operation Smile. You may be a surgeon who actually gives of your time and abilities to serve in one of these missions. You may be a donor who helps in the overall costs of performing these surgeries to bring a sparkle of hope and life and love to another person. What is important to remember is that these diamond values transform lives, restore human dignity, and give hope to the hopeless. This is where people shine brightest.

LIFE PRINCIPLE: NOT ALL VALUES ARE EQUAL

As a philanthropic leader, you will discover that not all values are equal. Some values you will place a higher priority to, or give more time to. You may value an efficient and effective charity more than a largely known charity that has more employees and overhead than necessary. As a person who makes substantial financial contributions to charities, you have most likely realized that there is a reason why certain charities want to spend so much time getting to know you; they value your money. Furthermore, they want to ensure that you are committed to their organization for life, or even thereafter when you plan to leave a portion of your estate to charity. Having the discernment to know the priority or even the hierarchy of your values is critical to making sound decisions as a philanthropic leader. Do you simply give money to an organization because your neighbor wants you to? Surely, you do not want to disappoint your friend by not participating in his or her favorite charity? Or do you give only to organizations that truly have your heart? When you find your values in tension, this is where understanding their particular place helps clarify the situation.

LIFE PRINCIPLE: DIFFERENT SITUATIONS DEMAND DIFFERENT LEADERSHIP

That is why it is imperative to be crystal clear about your values. For your values guide your decisions, shape your thinking, and ultimately reflect your character to others. Different situations will demand different values to rise to the top, while others may fade in the background. But this does not mean that you are living in an inauthentic manner or you are being a hypocrite. It simply means that you understand that different situations call for different leadership. You may value being on time and maintaining timely meetings, but if you engage in global philanthropic initiatives, then you will quickly understand that most parts of the world do not value time management the same as Americans. As you realize cultural differences as well as similarities between values, your leadership understanding becomes fuller, more complete and holistic. By being clearer about your values, and those you work among, you will improve how you relate to others by understanding why they do what they do and why you do what you do.

Because values often reveal why you do what you do, the more clear you are about your values, the better understanding and personal fulfillment you will have in your leadership as a philanthropist. Simply doing good deeds for goodness sake is too vague and will leave you frustrated. You cannot make a financial donation to each organization that asks, serve on every board, and go on every vision trip to see the work of philanthropy in action. You cannot attend every gala ball or participate in every fundraising drive and be as effective as you would like. Often donors continue to be bombarded daily by giving requests and other fundraising events. At first, you may have found these to be fun and joyful opportunities, a golf tournament here, a walk-a-thon there, a black tie this Friday night, and an opportunity to serve on another civic nonprofit board. But after awhile, you realize your life and leadership is being directed more by other people's values than your own. When this occurs, it is time to revaluate your values.

Re-evaluating your values may be something you want to do individually or with your spouse and family. If you have a family foundation, then each member of the family serving on the foundation should come together to participate collectively on the values of your foundation. What causes are important to you? What do your children value as being important? Are you living these values out as a family? Does each member have a particular role he or she can play within the foundation to not only *be* a part, but also *feel* a part of the work and mission? What values have you let go of that you need to regain in your life? And what values have slipped into your thinking and character without you even being aware? By asking yourself and/or your family the tough questions of values, you will begin to take control of the future you want to lead others into.

Your philanthropic leadership will begin to take on a sense of stability and courage when you revaluate your values, when you regain a sense of what is important. For you will then have a firm foundation of what you give to, where you want to serve, and how you want to participate with others along the journey. You will have a new sense of courage to say no to other giving and serving opportunities that do not align with your values without feeling guilty. You will have the courage and boldness to participate with others at a deeper level, because your values, your heart, and your core identity will be in alignment. You will begin to live out of who you are, rather than trying to please others. As a result, the depths of your leadership, giving, and overall sense of worth will begin to take on new meaning and purpose as you live and lead by your core values. You will experience the power, freedom, and energy of values in your life.

This power, freedom and energy emerging from value living, should not be taken lightly as simply a warm, fuzzy feeling you get, but rather it should be part of your core strategy as a philanthropic leader. Several years ago, I was drowning in donor requests from charitable organizations all over the world. Our name was out as a "soft touch" for giving. Historically, the foundation I served on gave generously to numerous different charities, churches, and missions. And one day I came to the board and said we must redefine what important tasks this foundation should execute. We cannot do it all and we do not want to continue to give financially to other organizations that we simply no longer value. Change was needed, and it began with our values. By reducing our values to two different categories, we were able to create clarity, which gives us a strategic edge. One category consists of the values that we desire, as a foundation, to support; for example, we value widows, orphans, the poor and oppressed. Therefore, our foundation financially supports and works along with other organizations that work directly with widows, orphans, the poor and the oppressed. Within this approach we have a three-tiered focus: local, national, and global. We value working with a children's home that is within five minutes from our house. We also value helping and serving other organizations that impact different geographical places in America. In addition, as a result of the enormity of problems in places like Africa, we work along side organizations that have operations, orphanages, and others points of impact in the developing world that carry out our values.

Then, the second category of our values pertains to our internal operations of a private family foundation. This entails everything from having next to zero overhead and operational expenses, while maximizing our funds and operations. For example, once I have traveled with an organization on a vision trip to see the work they do, then I do not need to travel with the same organization each and every year simply for the joys of taking another trip to observe; however, if there is a strategic way that I can help an organization's overseas staff, which may entail teaching leadership skills, then I may choose to go and give in that particular way. The point is that we want to run our foundation like an effective and efficient business that can actually increase its investments, while making a true difference in the lives of others.

As a result of clarifying our values and making these values known, it has become much easier as a board to make decisions that are in alignment with both our values and mission statement. It also creates a benchmark for money managers, investors, and other financial advisors. When these individuals realize that our foundation does not tolerate being charged excessively, and that we expect nice returns, even in the face of a recession, then our values highlight what we expect from both the board and contractual employees. When your values create expectations, then results can be measured both quantitatively and qualitatively. The monthly quantitative measurements of financial statements to the yearly qualitative measurements of helping widows, orphans, the poor and oppressed come from taking the time to revaluate values.

Another value our foundation finds helpful is creating a criterion of values for each board member. The values that your board members have will ultimately make or break your foundation and/or charity. There are many boards that have undergone extreme pain and anguish and even legal action because members of the board maintained opposing values. The criterion of values that my foundation holds is nicely summed up in an acrostic: VIRAL.

Each board member must have the same *vision* and *values* of the organization. If a candidate for our foundation cannot do this, he or she will not be asked to join our board. It often takes time to truly know if someone really believes in the vision and values of your foundation, and this is why your initiative as a philanthropic leader is ultimately to get to know others through a relationship, for only in a committed relationship will you know if a particular person would make a good candidate as a board member. The next letter, *I*, stands for *intellectual capital*. In other words, we value that our board members not only be smart, but also that they can bring some particular expertise to the foundation. For example, we have had an accountant, a money manager, and a strategic planner to serve on our board. Third, we expect and value *righteousness*. The character of each board member is marked by an ethical, moral, and righteous life. Fourth, we expect and value our board members to be *active* participants with the foundation. Besides attending all board meetings, they are also expected to actively contribute some skill, expertise, or talent to the many organizations our foundation serves. For example, one gentleman conducted a three-day strategic planning session for a children's home that our foundation supports. Our foundation does not simply write blank checks without being personally involved to see the success of the recipients throughout their entire journey. We all participate in an active role, in some capacity, to be part of the end results. Finally, we value *life capital*. Life capital simply means the wisdom, tacit knowledge, and acumen that come from living. As a result, the majority of our board members are older and wiser, and they are experienced leaders in their respective fields. Your board may not look like ours, but this is an example of how your values shape and inform the criterion of selecting board members.

You may need to go into more depth in regard to other values that impact your organization. In other words, do you value a diversity of perspectives on your board? If so, then your board members should reflect diversity. Do you value the benefits of a yearly or tri-yearly rotating board? Do you value an open, honest discussion over difficult board decisions, or do you value the positive reaffirmation of "groupthink"? Your values are vital to the success of your philanthropy. Your values matter, because your values influence your leadership, organization, and legacy.

AUTHENTICATING YOUR VALUES

If your values are not real, then your ability to lead will be weakened. People know when you are being true and authentic to your values. It is not just what you espouse to value, and the tonality you use, but also how you model those values in both good and difficult times. When life goes well, many leaders find that temptation rises to compromise their values. It is here where they become slack in the work, focus, and integrity of their beliefs. Likewise, when times are difficult, it is easy to be tempted to compromise your values for quick fixes. It is often easy to pick up the phone and make the necessary calls to usher in solutions to appease pressure from others. Unfortunately, in the world of philanthropy, band-aid solutions never address root problems. It is easy for celebrities to use their star power to quickly raise funds for Katrina victims of New Orleans and the Gulf Coast, but history continues to prove that several years past, the emotional sensational hype to raise funds do not address many of the issues that were only exposed from Hurricane Katrina.

Remember, your values define who you are and what you are about. Values give you clarity in the midst of chaos. Values shape your leadership, your life, and all of your relationships. In community, it is important that your values align with those whom you serve. Your values also simplify your life.

As a philanthropic leader, I rarely value money as the first solution to an apparent need. I know the enormous burden of hearing about and seeing so much need, and then the quick answer, if we only had x number of dollars, then we would meet all of these needs. And many of the eyes in the room turn and look at me, as if I were a bank. I am not a bank. You are not a bank.

Your values shape the type of scope you will have as a philanthropic leader. Values tell you what is important and what is not important. Values inform leaders, followers, organizational objectives, decisions and relationships. In order for philanthropic leadership to successfully make a difference, the leader's awareness of his or her values is critical. As Socrates believed "the unexamined life is not worth living," likewise, "you must have a set of values that speak loudly in your actions. This starts with the examined life."[15] The philanthropic leader understands the examined life begins when "your values shape your definition of importance."[16]

VALUES DEFINE CHARACTER

One major reason values bring clarity is that values are held hierarchically. In other words, some are more important than others no matter what the situation demands. On the other hand, some values shift to higher levels of priority depending on the situation. When two or more values come into conflict, between right and right, leaders find themselves in what Joseph Badaracco calls "defining moments." Here, "a defining moment, however, challenges us in a deeper way by asking us to choose between two or more ideals in which we deeply believe."[17] For instance, how do you choose between two very important needs? You can only fund one. When I was in Haiti serving from the aftermath of the earthquake, the needs were tremendous and continue to be. Since you cannot make everything happen at once, you will be faced with defining moments of where to give. Does our group purchase the generator, or do you help fund a wall that needs repairing? Both are critical, but only one can be chosen. This creates a defining moment between two options representing highly held beliefs and values. Badaracco elaborates:

> We form our character in defining moments because we commit to irreversible courses of action that shape our personal and professional identities. We reveal something new about us to ourselves and others because defining moments uncover something that had been hidden or crystallize something that had been only partially known. And we test ourselves because we discover whether we will live up to our personal ideals or only pay them lip service.[18]

If we form our character in defining moments, then the character of the leader will ultimately manifest itself in relation to the philanthropic community. In recent years, the character of philanthropic leaders in both public and private foundations reveals greed, hidden agendas, selfishness, and other character traits not becoming of ethical practices. From Bernie Madoff's Ponzi scheme to sibling rivalries over family foundations, examples like these are too often nearer to you than you might think. For too long good character has been assumed as a trait for philanthropists, but in today's world of big ego giving, lawsuits, and self-promotion, good character can no longer be assumed in the world of philanthropy.

LEADERSHIP EXERCISE

1. As you ponder your values, make a list of your top ten life values. These are the people, places, practices, purposes, and things in your life that you hold most dear.
2. Make a list of values you aspire to live by.
3. Describe a time in your life where you were faced with a defining moment. What was at stake? What did you choose? How did your decision impact you?
4. What do you value the most in regard to your work as a philanthropist?
5. How do you prioritize your values, and practice them in such a way that others realize the authenticity of them?

LEADING IN ALIGNMENT

*To attain inner peace you must actually give your life, not
just your possessions. When you at last give your life—
bringing into alignment your beliefs and the way you live
then, and only then, can you begin to find inner peace.*
—Peace Pilgrim

Leading in alignment is absolutely essential for philanthropic
leadership. Without alignment, your leadership will suffer a loss of focus
and clarity, and the inner peace that comes from life balance. Just as
driving your car with a tire out of alignment causes unnecessary wear
and tear, so too leading out of alignment brings unnecessary problems.
Leading with alignment means your values, beliefs, hopes and dreams are
in focus and proper perspective to where your heart is and to where you
spend your time, energy and money. Leading with alignment means you
have an understanding of your relationships and how your priorities reflect
those relationships.

> ## LEADERSHIP PRINCIPLE: IT'S NOT ABOUT
> ## MY WAY OR THE HIGHWAY

Alignment begins with your spoken and unspoken assumptions,
beliefs, thoughts, and values. Once you are clear on what you passionately
care about, the people in your life, and where you want to go, then it is
your responsibility to keep on track. Staying focused on your core purposes
as a philanthropic leader is tough work. Once you are known within your
community and circle of influence as one who desires to serve and give
and make a difference, then organizations, friends, and family will come
from all corners seeking your help. It is here where you must access each
situation, each cause, and each request to see if it falls within alignment.
It is not enough that an organization needs your help. Your values should
align with the organization's values. But even if you find alignment in like
values, you may still not have the necessary alignment within your heart.
This feeling may leave after time, and you may find that all is good as you
move forward in partnership with others. Or you may discover the more

69

time you spend with certain people, causes, and charities, the more out of alignment you are with your core values. It is here that stepping away may be needed.

There will be times in your life when a real perceived need comes to your attention. You may have even dreamed of participating in seeking a solution to this need, and now you find yourself with the opportunity to give. Being excited that other like-minded individuals also want to become involved in a relationship to fulfill a certain need, you eagerly jump on the bandwagon to participate. The need could be anything from restoring a public library to creating a public park. Whatever the project is, if it fits with your values and beliefs and other people desire to join the cause, then the excitement builds. This is good as long as everyone gets what they believe should occur, but in the real world that rarely happens. One may want to build a park in memory of their loved one and be the primary donor, while others may want a larger donor and participant base and make it a memorial for the troops serving in Iraq. When the secondary and tertiary issues arise, you may find yourself feeling a little out of alignment.

As this occurs, it is important to realize that your leadership should not necessarily take the "my way or the highway" approach. You need to go deeper in relationship with the parties you feel somewhat out of alignment with. You may need to clarify what is important now that you are out of alignment.

CLARIFYING WHAT'S IMPORTANT NOW

It was approximately one month before the 2008 Ryder Cup would take place in Louisville, Kentucky when United States team captain Paul Azinger met with Coach Lou Holtz to discuss successful leadership planning. One nugget of wisdom that came from the dinner meeting was Holtz's strategic clarifying tool: *WIN—What's Important Now?* This particular tool along with many others implemented by Azinger and the United States team gave victory over the European team. Knowing what's important now brings clarity to your leadership as well.

In the days after 9/11, many CEOs, presidents, executive directors, and board members had to respond quickly to how the attacks on America would impact their organizational health. With a quick decline in donations, many organizations did not have crisis management strategies. As a result, the lack of foresight and proper leadership caused many nonprofits to suffer more than necessary.

When outside forces occur in the world, be it hurricanes or the current economic meltdown, being able to clarify what is important now is essential as your leadership adapts to the larger context. When I was in Haiti, we had a perimeter wall that came crashing down as we were there with the children. Many of the children immediately started screaming, crying, and being totally terrorized as if another earthquake was occurring. Even though the wall came crashing down due to some construction taking place and not an earthquake, the organization had to immediately make the necessary decisions to secure the perimeter where so many orphans were staying. By evening, this group had United Nations' security, which guarded the children throughout the night. This of course was not on the leadership's agenda for the day, but when life happens, you must be prepared to respond quickly and wisely.

How you respond to a major reduction in your financial portfolio or your giving habits, will reveal to others what you believe to be necessary now that you find yourself in a new situation. Philanthropic leaders who respond to each obstacle, emergency, or wild card event that occurs by clarifying what's important now create a context of confidence in the midst of chaos.

Earlier this year, a friend of mine was laid off from a nonprofit organization that had recently hired him. After what appeared to be a typical ninety-day trail period for employment, the executive director made it clear that this particular employee was great for their organization, but that they simply could not keep him on payroll as a result of America's current economic crisis. As the nonprofit's income from donations declined, the organization had to cut budgets and layoff employees. From my personal involvement with this group and their executive leadership, I believe they should have clearly seen the indicators three months before, and new employees should not have been hired. This situation prompted the questions, "Are they oblivious about the world in which they serve, or were they dishonest in regard to laying off certain individuals?" Either way, it is hard to lead with integrity when you are not able to honestly clarify what is important each and every day.

There will be times in your philanthropic leadership where positive events occur. These events may range from generating millions of dollars from the sale of a business to being invited to open your public charity in new countries that once prohibited your involvement. When life quickly changes, you must be ready to adapt and change with it. This requires you to define where your foundation is, where it wants to go, and if a new positive opportunity will accelerate your progress. Your ability to clarify each major decision provides you with the ability to understand which external opportunities will accelerate your goals and purposes while adapting appropriately.

LEADERSHIP EXERCISE

1. How do you feel when you know you are out of alignment with your values?
2. Have you implemented the "my way or the highway" approach to your philanthropy? If so, describe what happened. How did you get there?
3. Decide how often you need to revaluate your current position. Weekly? Monthly? Yearly? How often do you need to realign your philanthropic compass?
4. Ask yourself: what is important now? How might the *WIN* strategy help your philanthropic initiatives?
5. Describe a time when you felt out of alignment with a particular charity. How did it make you feel?

THE VALUE OF PARTICIPATION

The poor must have a chance to participate in
decision-making that affects their lives.
—Muhammad Yunus

A participatory worldview is an emerging and collaborative approach to knowledge, action, and human development. This worldview "is an emerging worldview, more holistic, pluralist and egalitarian, which is essentially participative," claims Peter Reason of the University of Bath.[19] Within a participatory worldview, the following concepts arise:

- Reality is subjective-objective, which means people bring a multitude of perspectives (subjective) to real problems and concerns (objective).
- Knowledge emerges from many sources including, but not limited to, the following:
  1. Experiential knowing is through direct face-to-face encounter with a person, place or thing; it is knowing through empathy and resonance, and is almost impossible to put into words.
  2. Presentational knowing emerges from experiential knowing, and provides its first expression through forms of imagery such as poetry and story, drawing, sculpture, movement, dance and so on.
  3. Propositional knowing "about" something, is knowing through ideas and theories, and is expressed in abstract language or mathematics.
  4. Practical knowing is knowing "how to" do something and is expressed in a skill, knack, or competence.
- Research is something people do together to solve problems of concern to them.
- In a participative worldview the purpose of knowledge is practical: human flourishing in its widest sense, which entails the values of being human.

- And finally, a spiritual dimension arises from a participatory worldview.[20]

A participatory worldview brings action. Reason believes the research learned from participatory action is best applied if "used throughout the world to work with people who are disadvantaged or oppressed as a way both to help them solve practical problems and also to reclaim their capacity to create their own knowledge."[21] If your organization is the coalition for the homeless, then you may want to implement a practical participatory worldview by actively having a qualified homeless person serve on your board. Or you may have a homeless person make board appearances to give real insight, foresight, and feedback on what works and what does not work. By allowing such an individual to actively participate alongside the other board members, then you as a leader and board will be better positioned to truly understand core issues that a financial statement will not give you. In addition, you may want to experience homelessness for a twenty-four or forty-eight hour period. With no cell phone and no money, you and a friend may want to truly feel homelessness as you stand on a street corner or sleep under a bridge or stay in a homeless shelter for a night or two. Of course, it may be dangerous, but many groups in the past have safely held participatory experiences like this. Likewise, if your organization consists of a children's home or an orphanage, then it would only make sense to have board members who are either mature current teenage children whom can participate or even individuals whom once were orphans themselves have a place on your board. The key is to look for multiple ways to gain knowledge that benefits the people you serve by having them participate in dispensing that knowledge. In addition, with multiple perspectives you will be in a better position when faced with decisions as a philanthropic leader.

PARTICIPATORY ACTION MAKES A DIFFERENCE

Philanthropic leadership opens the door for participatory action. It is one thing to simply maintain a theoretical worldview, and quite another to put it into practice. Participatory action in and of itself sounds great on paper, but when you actually act on it, then and only then, are you beginning to lead others to flourish. By leading people to flourish, "one aim is to produce knowledge and action directly useful to a group of people— through research, through adult education, and through sociopolitical action."[22] These examples are focused on the people you are serving, rather than, simply serving your own assumptions, agendas, and programs. When the focus of philanthropic leadership is on the people and their needs, rather than simply raising and distributing funds, then the leadership takes on an others-focused approach to empowerment.

When your leadership focuses on other people, then you are ready to empower your followers to action. Hence, "The second aim is to empower people at a second and deeper level through the process of constructing and using their own knowledge."[23] If a charity is going to help the poor, for example, then "the poor must have a chance to participate in decision making that affects their lives."[24] This personal empowerment becomes a strategic advantage for the philanthropic leader because the best strategy is to let the poor, for example, have the power, skills, and knowledge to lift themselves out of their own need for charity. And it is here, that an authentic and collaborative spirit arises within the philanthropic leader to empower the poor with what they need, rather than simply giving another handout. This relationship, then, is established in the cultural traditions of the people you serve. Or stated differently, the philanthropic leader is to "go to the people, live among them, learn from them, and love them. Start with what they know, build on what they have."[25]

This type of leadership relies on the basic foundations of participatory action research. Within the worldview of participatory action, comes philanthropic knowledge for the people. In other words, the outcomes of action are not to primarily benefit and highlight the endearment of the leader, but rather "the primary outcome of all these forms of inquiry is a change in the lived experiences of those involved in the inquiry."[26] Thus, both the leader and followers undergo transformation. This transformation fueled by humble relationships, action, and trust aligns with philanthropic thinking, which is the heartbeat of action science:

> Participants are empowered to define their world in the service of what they see as worthwhile interests, and as a consequence they change their world in significant

ways, through action—building a road to their village, developing a new form of holistic medical practice—and through experience—developing a sense of empowerment and competence.[27]

For example, LEGS (LeTourneau Empowering Global Solutions) from LeTourneau University (www.legsresearch.org) creates sustainable solutions for the developing world when it comes to prosthetic technologies for amputees. Rather than simply sending prosthetic legs to men, women, and children all around the world, when disaster strikes like in Haiti, the LEGS organization empowers local nationals to be able to create and fit their own people with prosthetics rather than on waiting for the technology to come in the mail. This not only gives nationals their own knowledge systems, but it also improves their healthcare, while allowing for children to continually be fitted quickly for prosthetics as they continue to grow. This nonprofit organization truly engages in participatory action, while giving dignity, creating sustainability, and meeting true needs from the ground up.

When participatory actions like this occur, it helps prevent the danger of elite leadership, because the people participate in their own philanthropic change. Typically, "the fallacy is to assume that because I have studied and lived in a society that somehow wound up with prosperity and peace, I know enough to plan for other societies to have prosperity and peace."[28] Unfortunately, this type of arrogance permeates philanthropic leadership, which is why "the people paying the bills are rich people who have very little knowledge of poor people."[29] As a result, Yunus and others continue to show how "charity creates a one-sided power relationship," where the rich power their agenda onto those they are attempting to help.[30] Reason claims, "movements for social change are normally led by intellectuals who are in a position to provide leaders not because of any particular aptitude but because they are privileged by their economic and social status."[31] Besides a tipped scale of power, the danger of charitable acts among elite leadership brings long-term harm. For example, research reveals the following:

Take away any initiative and responsibility from people. If people know that things can be received "free," they tend to spend their energy and skill chasing the "free" things rather than using the same energy and skill to accomplish things on their own. Handouts encourage dependence rather than self-help and self-confidence.[32]

This trend created "the greatest tragedy of post-World War II society—the donor-recipient relationship," claims philanthropist Susan Raymond.[33] She elaborates:

> By conceiving of and treating individuals (or organizations or even entire nations) as "recipients," we should not be surprised that this is how they begin to think of themselves. Hence, creating self-reliance is predictably difficult. The recipient receives from the donor. Therein lies the tragedy. The very approach creates dependency.[34]

In addition, "handouts also encourage corruption. When aid monies are donated to help the poor, the officials who are in charge of distributing the free goods and services often turn themselves, and their favored friends, into the first beneficiaries of the program."[35] Roger Sandberg, a friend of mine spent 5 years in Sudan, working as a philanthropic leader, where he saw food distribution to the extreme poor being stolen by oppressors once the presence of safety was out of sight. Even though he is now with MedAir (www.medair.org), an emergency relief and rehabilitation NGO, he understands the dire need of actually being where you serve. When you actually go to places like Indonesia, Haiti, or Darfur, then you can actually participate with the people you are trying to help, serve, and love. And only then, are you in a position to help reduce many of the unnecessary tragedies of food being stolen, wasteful giving occurring, and other loses that you cannot see when you simply make a financial donation.

LEADERSHIP EXERCISE

1. Describe how you believe an inclusive participatory action committee might benefit your philanthropic initiatives.

2. How can your leadership involve the recipients of your philanthropic projects to embrace their own ability to create systems, strategies, and knowledge that empower them to succeed?

3. Does your philanthropic leadership create dependency or self-reliance? How?

4. What action steps do you need to apply today in order to create a participatory environment with the people you work with?

5. How do you need to change as a leader in order to bring about change in others?

CHAPTER THREE:
THE ESSENTIALS OF LEADING

This is my command: Love each other.
—Jesus

WHEN YOU ARE COMMITTED TO loving others, you will be committed to listening to what is in their heart and on their mind. And when you listen to the heart and mind of the ones you love, then you are in a position to learn from them. As you learn what they truly need, you are in a better posture to bring liberation from the bondage they are in. When the liberation comes, then you can join them in celebrating a life of leading a legacy. The command to love each other that Jesus gave is simple yet profoundly foundational. For without love, you will not listen well, nor will you learn what you need, or bring about the liberation required to lift others up in a spirit of philanthropy.

LOVING —THE FOUNDATION OF LEADERSHIP

Can you love people and lead them without imposing your will?
—Tao

Leadership is not about you. It is not about your agenda, your power, your position, your great abilities and resources. Leadership is not even about your dream. When life is all about you and your desires and wishes, then that is not leadership, it is selfishness. Leadership that is selfish in nature is not only destructive, but it often ends in isolation. And if a leader does not have followers, then leadership ceases to exist.

The same is true for philanthropic leadership. Philanthropic leadership is not about you, the donor, how much money you have, how much power you can demonstrate, or what your every wish and desire is. Historically, philanthropic leadership is all about the biggest donor using his or her money to create the biggest name by erecting tall buildings, statues, and other symbols of power and prestige. Even though society uses many of these buildings from libraries to music halls, to hospital wings, the amount of resources required to maintain these structures continues to create burdens on future generations. While Americans spend more money and go more into debt, all we are doing is adding burden upon burden to the future generations, while we often live for our own self-indulgent lives. This is not what leadership is about.

Leadership is about love. Loving others is the foundation of leadership. Without love, your leadership will not sustain itself. And love ensures that future generations have the necessary skills, knowledge, and wisdom to properly handle the resources, projects, and buildings that philanthropists initiate today. Many people have inherited great wealth, homes, and businesses without the proper training, tools, and wisdom to handle these assets. As a result, often money is quickly wasted, homes go into foreclosure, and businesses fail. The same is true for philanthropic giving. For giving to truly be a blessing rather than a burden, it must be accompanied with the necessary empowerment, education, skills, and intelligence for long-term sustainability. Long-term sustainability, growth, and human flourishing occur best where there is love.

On February 14, 2008, Bono, along with Sotheby's of New York, hosted the "All You Need is Love" auction to raise money and awareness for the United Nations Foundation to support HIV/AIDS relief programs in Africa. Love was definitely in the air that Valentine's Day evening, along with the more than $42 million that was raised. But this was not just another auction with donated artwork; rather, the pieces auctioned were targeted around the theme of love. Bono told the auction attendees, "We only want you to buy what you love because love is what (RED) is all about."[4] Product (RED) is about loving others, loving the poorest of the poor in Africa to help reduce the spreading of preventable and treatable diseases. And it appears that groups like Product (RED) and DATA (Debt, Aids, Trade, Africa), now under the One Campaign, love the people they serve, love the people they recruit, and they are primarily driven to do what they do because of love.

The *Bible* communicates that love and giving go hand-in-hand: *for God so loved, that he gave.* Love is the fuel for giving. While in Haiti with so many of the newly orphans from Port-au-Prince, it became clear that they could not speak English and I could not speak Creole. But we both knew how to speak the language of love. And love powerfully transcends language as it speaks to the heart. All the children I would play with, help walk if they were newly amputees, feed, and simply love, only wanted love. They did not beg for money, and they did not want anything except to be held, hugged, and helped. And love filled their hearts and my heart as we connected heart to heart without being able to otherwise communicate.

Love gives you the opportunity to be a joyful, excited, and delightful philanthropist. As scripture also claims, if you give all that you have to the poor, but have not love, then your giving experience is soured.[5] This souring effect often impacts you, the donor, and the recipient. And when this occurs, it eventually becomes clear that your love is not in a particular project, people, or purpose. Just as you are tempted to purchase what you love, the same is true to where you give.

---

4 Available from http://blog.joinred.com/2008/02/all-you-need-is-love-special-red-art.html; Internet; accessed 15 February 2008.
5 See I Corinthians 13:3.

Your love for giving, for helping others, for doing the work of philanthropy in a meaningful and significant way should reveal your care for the work, and also for the individuals you engage with. This means that it is a priority to get to know the people on your board, your team, your projects, and also those who receive the primary benefit from your philanthropic initiatives. This takes time, energy, and a heart of love. The people you serve alongside will quickly know if you genuinely care for their well-being. Several years ago, I was in Kenya meeting with government leaders, non-governmental organization (NGO) workers, and men, women, and children who have experienced horrific oppression, violence, and harm. One particular orphaned boy glowed with love. As I spent an afternoon with him, it was evident that all of the money, aid, and resources alone cannot bring love into the life of another person. Only a person willing to give love actually brings love into the life of another. When this occurs, both the donor and recipient receive an intangible heart blessing. Where there is love, peace floods the heart and room, and hope begins to bloom. For money, resources, and other forms of philanthropic aid come and go, but the loving impact you can make on those you serve as a leader can and will last a lifetime. Love bridges the distance between defeat and perseverance, hopelessness and hope, and in times of difficulty, the memory of love provides the courage to press onward. It is a shared blessing between philanthropic leaders and the people they touch.

LIFE PRINCIPLE: IF YOUR LOVE IS NOT AUTHENTIC, THEN YOUR LEADERSHIP WILL SUFFER

Several years ago, I had the sacred privilege to visit a genocide site in Rwanda where over five thousand Tutsi men, women, and children were slaughtered to death with machetes during the 1994 genocide that tortured and killed over a million people in approximately one hundred days. A chilling quiver went through my body as I stood in a small church house where these men, women, and children gathered for fear of their lives. Bones, skulls, decaying clothes, and a few rusty possessions surrounded me as I pictured these mothers and fathers, brothers and sisters, whole families who were slaughtered to death. Seeing this showed to me the type of horrific leadership that can occur where there is no love. As the team of philanthropists, NGO leaders, and others gathered the next day with President Paul Kagame, we were all moved once again by his genuine love for the people of Rwanda. It is this love for others that compels him to initiate a movement of forgiveness, healing, and hope by a country that still suffers from recent terror.

In ancient China, Lao-tzu gave the Chinese people the *Tao Te Ching*: pronounced (Dow Deh Jing) otherwise known as *The Book of the Way*. From this ancient Chinese wisdom comes the question, "Can you love people and lead them without imposing your will?"[36] This question has enormous ramifications of what it means to be a philanthropic leader. Jesus exemplified this type of leadership when He engaged all kinds of people with all kinds of needs. His love allowed Him to engage people at their level, rather than demanding that they come to His. His leadership of love understood that there would be times where He loved others, like the rich young ruler, who would walk away sad[6]. In other words, Jesus did not impose his will, yet loved and led instead.

This type of love that drove Jesus to the cross is what theologians call kenosis. Kenosis is an emptying of oneself for the greater good of another. Or in terms of philanthropy, the kenotic donor gives not to receive name recognition, more power, or prestige. Jesus had multiple sources He could have tapped into and used for His own personal benefit, but rather He emptied Himself giving us an example of humble love. A kenotic style of giving draws the high net worth donor out of his or her ivory tower office of modern comforts to actually get to know those he or she is serving. This kenotic love opens the door for authentic relationships to occur between the donor and recipient. And from such humility comes the understanding that love is patient, love is kind as portrayed in the famous Biblical discourse on love. In I Corinthians 13, the love depicted illustrates a model for philanthropic leadership. Your leadership and work as a philanthropist will take enormous amounts of time. Whether you are trying to find a cure for HIV/AIDS, malaria, breast cancer, reform the public education in America, reduce infant mortality in developing countries, introduce micro-financing to the poor, or simply improve the city in which you live, your patience will be tested. As it is tested, will you

---

6 See Luke 18:18–23.

continue to lead others with kindness? Will you lead with the power of love that gives you the ability to truly make a difference?

In 1997, *Slate* magazine started to publish America's biggest philanthropic donors of the year. Like *Forbes*, which annually publishes the wealthiest people in the world, *Slate* opened the doors for philanthropists to be challenged by others to give more. This came about primarily with Ted Turner, the founder of CNN news, who gave $1 billion to the United Nations as a way to challenge his fellow billionaires to step up to the plate and give. Of course, Mr. Turner received lots of publicity and scrutiny for this type of public display, but nevertheless, he planted a seed in the mind of other billionaires. This challenge and appeal to one's pride to give more appears to be a good healthy form of philanthropic competition; however, it could lead to envy, which is dangerous within philanthropic circles. One of the more important dangers of envy that occurs in philanthropy is the danger of foundations not partnering with one another. When envy cumulates with pride, numerous organizations will attempt to solve the same problem without sharing information, ideas, dead end solutions, resources, and relationships. This occurs often within scientific research initiatives for programs seeking cures for breast cancer. But this same spirit of envy is also felt among many NGOs working only miles apart to help the poor in places like Uganda. You will encounter many great organizations that could all benefit not only from each other, but they could also make a greater impact on the work if they would remove the envy and begin to embrace a cooperative relationship for the common good.

Another danger of envy comes when you feel like you don't have enough money, name power, or a large enough network to make things happen as quickly as other philanthropists or charitable organizations. It is your responsibility as a leader to stop pride and envy from creeping into your heart, thoughts, and relationships both internally and externally to your foundation or organization. Philanthropic leadership celebrates all successes and rejoices with others.

With this loving attitude, you should not boast about your giving to receive the praises of your peers, but rather tell your story in a way that encourages, inspires, and challenges others to join you as a philanthropic leader. Just as love does not boast, it also does not take pride in its lofty position.

As the love description from I Corinthians 13 goes, the philanthropic leader is not rude, self-seeking, or easily angered, and keeps no records of wrong. But rather, philanthropic leaders rejoice where there is truth, knowing that a posture of authentic, genuine love always protects those they serve: love trusts, it hopes, and it perseveres. In other words, it is not about you and your agenda, but rather philanthropic leadership is about a loving participatory relationship for the betterment of others. You do have a responsibility to learn from mistakes and to use those as future guideposts. But in the process, you should not badger others in an effort to bring about human flourishing. And, you have the obligation to seek truthful, honest feedback and measurements that give you and others reliable data to both qualify and quantify your work. This type of love seeks to truly make a difference for others.

Finally, the Biblical passage communicates the beautiful essence of what it means to be a philanthropic leader: "When I was a child, I talked like a child, I thought like a child, I reasoned like a child. When I became a man, I put childish ways behind me."[7] Philanthropic leadership is maturity. It is being responsible for the decisions you make for others and alongside others. It is saying you have enough money, toys, and trinkets of this world, and now you are ready to make a difference for others. The maturity of philanthropic leadership begins with loving others enough to enter into their world to empower them. It realizes there is more to life than making more money, exercising more power, and living a self-indulgent lifestyle. Like United Nations' goodwill ambassador, Angelina Jolie, your love compels you to sit in the dust, dirt, and muck, under the unbearable heat from the African sky, to listen, to engage and love refugees, widows, orphans, the poor and oppressed. This takes maturity. This takes leadership. This takes love.

So what does your leadership of love look like? Is it self-centered or others-centered? Does it envy or does it join hands in partnership with others to make a difference? Does it allow you to think thoughts outside of your religious tradition, worldview, and subculture? Has your leadership of love taken you to the point of saying, "I don't have all the answers, but I'm willing to keep learning and growing." Have you chosen to love another by emptying yourself of your own pride, agenda, and manipulation? In

7 I Corinthians 13:11, *New International Version*.

order to truly excel at giving, you must be willing to love. Are you? Are you willing to absorb the awesome riches and wealth of knowing the poor? Are you willing to receive from the poor the powerful lessons of wisdom, life, and love that they give you?

Courage is required to embark on this journey to the foundation of philanthropy: the love of mankind. Philanthropic leadership takes courage to consider the ideas, cultural traditions, religious perspectives, and political ideologies of others to engage the poor on their level. It takes courage to set aside your business-as-usual mindset when serving people cross-culturally or next door. It takes courage to join hands in partnership with those whom you may have once considered your competitors. It takes courage to love. It takes courage to give. It takes courage to think outside the box. It takes courage to listen to new ideas. It takes courage to believe in a better future. It takes courage to lead. It takes courage to make a difference.

LEADERSHIP EXERCISE

1. What is the foundation of your leadership?
2. How does your leadership reveal love to others?
3. How do you lead others and love them without imposing your will?
4. How do you portray authentic leadership?
5. As a philanthropist, make a list of ways you can lead others with a spirit of love.

LISTENING—THEY KNOW MORE THAN YOU

*I remind myself every morning: Nothing I say this day will teach
me anything. So if I'm going to learn, I must do it by listening.*
—Larry King

Listening is love in action. When we listen, we communicate to others
that what they have to say is important. As a leader, the people you serve
know if you truly care about them by the degree to which you listen to
them. One of the biggest problems among charitable organizations is
that they do not utilize those they serve by listening to them. If your
organization supports inner city youth, then you should have one qualified
young person to serve on your board. If you cater to the homeless or
work with patients dying of HIV, then a key strategic ingredient to your
leadership is allowing certain individuals to actively contribute in decision
making as a fellow board member or advisor who truly understands the
issues, problems, and difficulties that your organization is attempting to
address.

LIFE PRINCIPLE: ENGAGE OTHERS BY LISTENING TO THEIR HEART

For too long, rich philanthropists, government leaders, and NGO
leaders believed that they knew what was best for those they were
serving. However, this leadership allowed no room for true inquiry. As a
philanthropic leader, you need to spend quality time observing, listening,
and engaging those you serve. And in order to do this well, you will need
to invest large amounts of time with those you serve. This may entail living
among the poor, moving to their neighborhood, and truly immersing your
soul in their culture, understanding their worldview and life. Or it may
mean that you spend one afternoon a week at the local hospital conversing
with cancer patients to define and prioritize the needs that your foundation
is attempting to solve. If you give money to breast cancer research, do
you know what it is like to have experienced breast cancer? Do you know

the needs of husbands who watched their wives go through enormous suffering? Do you know the daily needs, struggles, emotions, hopes and fears, and challenges that these patients endure? A way to understand those you and your philanthropy seek to serve is by being with these people in a relationship for the goal of simply listening.

A friend of mine, Ed Doyle, spends his Saturday mornings playing pick-up basketball with inner city youth. It is here where he learned that a large number of teenagers do not eat a square meal on the weekends. Many of these young people eat only while they are at school during the week. As a result, Doyle started a food backpack program. On Friday afternoons, the teenagers who participate are provided enough food to carry them till breakfast at school on Monday morning. This type of philanthropic leadership only comes when you begin to engage others where they are located.

LISTEN TO THE BOOKS YOU READ

As a philanthropic leader it is your responsibility to listen, learn, and grow as a leader. One place where listening, learning, and growing occurs is when you read a book, scan a magazine, or pick up on critical vital pulses in the media. Some books are filled with warm ideas of philanthropic initiatives, while others attempt to grapple with world poverty, global hunger, and other dire epidemic needs. You will never know what may spark your creative juices, spur you to action, and give you a deeper understanding of philanthropic issues if you do not take the time to listen to wisdom found in the books you read.

I just recently finished reading *The Hole in Our Gospel*, by Richard Stearns, president of World Vision, a global humanitarian NGO working with children in nearly 100 different countries. This particular book caught my heart, not only because of the great stories it tells, but also because it is filled with recent numerical data about everything from the amount of money given by Americans to the great epidemics that plague the developing world. Nevertheless, Stearns understands the need of how loving and listening go hand-in-hand for philanthropic leaders. Stearns writes:

The poor are not lab rats on whom we can experiment with our pet theories; they are human beings with rich cultural and personal stories of their own. They have hopes and dreams, tragedies and triumphs in their lives. They need us to love them first and then listen to them.[37]

When you listen to the books you read and learn from them, you will begin to build a wealth of knowledge, wisdom, and insight that will prove faithful to your philanthropic journey.

KNOWING YOUR CUSTOMER

Your foundation or charitable organization will find itself in a better position by listening to the customers. When you stop listening you begin to lose your ability to see reality. You may think you know the problems and concerns of your organization, but only until you truly listen to others and go where they are will you begin to regain a sense of reality. Often mental models that form and shape your beliefs and ideas about a particular subject block your ability to truly listen. It is when you deliberately engage those you serve, and truly get to know them, will you be able to listen and know your customer.

As I was consulting with a goodwill type of charity recently, it occurred to me that the leadership team of this particular nonprofit did not live among its customers. This group sells discounted used clothes, furniture, technology and a whole bunch of other donated merchandise to a lower class area. But what drives these people to come to your thrift store versus the one two blocks away? Besides the fact that your customer does not make a lot of money, what are they really looking for when they shop here? What do they need? And what could you provide to get customers to come in the door? Without going into the details of marketing, the simple fact remains: if you don't know your customer, if you do not truly listen to their heart, then you will not know why they do what they do. Once you do listen, you are in a better position to learn and provide them with what they need.

LISTEN TO YOUR ADVISORS

One of the greatest assets you will create as a philanthropic leader is a personal board of advisors consisting of men and women from whom you seek counsel, advice, and wisdom. Your advisors may include those who are on your family foundation's board or your charity's board, but these people are not simply board members who serve formally in a legally binding way. On the other hand, they serve you and your interests as a philanthropic leader. When you feel the burdens of giving, you can turn to these individuals to share the load. Or when you have ideas or strategies you desire feedback from, then these are the people you go to. Your personal board of advisors may consist of a trusted attorney or accountant. The point is that you need a group of trusted advisors who share the experiences of giving with you. From encouraging you with charities to invest in, charities to avoid, or strategies that work well, these men and women should bring honest feedback, a sharp intellect, and a passion to see others succeed on your journey.

LISTEN TO YOUR HEART

As a philanthropic leader, you must listen to your heart. There are more organizations than you will ever be able to join, more needs than you will ever be able to meet, and more problems than you will ever be able to solve. For the most part, charities do good work, are honest and ethical, and truly make a difference in the world. Because the needs are so much greater than you, your resources, and your circle of influence, you must practice listening to your heart.

Listening to your heart as a philanthropic leader is not an easy task and it takes practice to do it well. The heart can be easily deceived. It does pursue wrong things from time to time, and it can lead you down the wrong path as a leader. However, most leaders know when they are headed in a direction they should not be on. Some leaders stop listening to the warning signs of their heart. They ignore their inner conscience and attempt to do whatever they are being tempted to do in their own strength.

But when you listen to the pulses of your heart and when you coincide them with your conscience, then your heart is probably leading you in the right direction. You know when something does not add up. You know when a charity seeking funding or some other need seems to not make sense. Your heart knows when life seems to be out of alignment with your core values and beliefs. And the more questions you learn to ask, the more you probe into sticky matters, the more your heart will discern truth. So learn to listen to your heart, for it is the source of life, love, caution, courage, hope and inspiration.

STRATEGIC LISTENING

Strategic listening entails listening for what is not said as much as what is said. As you listen, ask probing questions to bring clarity to your understanding. You may also want to restate in your own words what you believed you heard embedded in a conversation with another person. This way, the other person may clarify if you have interpreted their meaning differently. Also, strategic listening entails listening from a contextual perspective. By understanding the greater context, background information, or where the other person is coming from, you are in a better position to lead. In addition, as you listen to the tonality used and facial expressions given, train yourself to listen to all the many nonverbal clues that exist in dialogue.

As you improve your strategic listening skills, continue to look for loopholes in conversations, ask the hard questions, and do not be afraid to seek clarity. By trusting your common sense, seek out sound thinking as you listen. Strategic listening takes time, intentionality, and a trained ear to lead well.

In summation, listening is love in action. When we listen, we tell those around us that they matter. As a leader, your followers will know if you truly love them by the way you listen. Listening takes time, energy, and an intense laser-like focus and attention to truly hear the heart of another. Listening is not simply something you exercise in conversation with another, but more importantly, listening should become a hallmark characteristic of your leadership. Listening is a way of living each and every moment intentionally. As you learn the art and skill of listening, you become aware of not only what is said, but also what is not said. The order in which words are presented, and the tonality in which words are spoken, will give you greater insight as a skilled listener.

LEADERSHIP EXERCISE

1. Commit to strategic listening as you engage with those around you.
2. Visit your local bookstore and scan the titles of philanthropy books or search for them on the web. Make a list of several books that pique your interest and commit to listening to what they tell you.
3. Ask your top three advisors how well you listen to them.
4. Describe a time when you did not listen to your heart. What happened? Did you have any regrets?
5. What is one thing you have learned from listening to someone who you did not previously believe could influence your thinking?

LEARNING—A RELATIONSHIP JOURNEY

Learning is not attained by chance, it must be sought
for with ardor and attended to with diligence.
—Abigail Adams

To lead is to learn and learning occurs when you begin to lead. In other words, leadership is a relationship journey where learning occurs within both the leader and follower. As a philanthropic leader, if your leadership is to improve, then you must become more than simply a donor of money. You must begin a relationship journey with those you seek to serve.

This journey begins with your call to become a philanthropic leader. As you respond to your call to this posture of serving for the good of others, then you are on the path of what it means to truly be a philanthropic leader. This journey is a love journey where your love opens the door to relationships. With love as the foundation and motivation fueling your work, you become aware of the need around you. As you practice the art of intentional listening, you will find yourself becoming an avid learner. As you learn about needs in your community, America, and the world at large, you will find yourself wanting to make a difference. And you will learn about both the blessings and burdens of being a philanthropic leader. As you continue your journey, you will continue to learn more about those whom you care for, and you will also learn more about your own neediness. This is where the paradox of learning occurs.

PARADOX OF LEARNING

Once you have been on this journey for some time, you will discover that you do not know it all. You do not have all the answers and some of the answers you thought you knew were wrong. You may have believed you had it all together, but realized you were not even asking the right questions. You will begin to see how those you initially targeted to serve and help have actually exposed to you how much you need help. This paradox of learning will turn your heart inside out, and your world upside down. Rather than being the big shot, you begin to see how desperate you are to learn and grow as a person.

The beauty of being in a learning relationship is that everyone gets an equal opportunity to learn. It is not simply that you are there to coach, mentor, and instruct those you lead without learning from them, but rather the relationship is open for participatory learning to occur. In this relationship journey, sometimes you are at the helm leading the way and other times you discover it is best to remain quiet by allowing someone else to step in and take charge. This does not mean that your organization, your philanthropic initiatives, or your overall vision constantly changes and that you find yourself in a chaotic organizational structure of leadership; on the contrary, this means you seek opportunities for learning. Sometimes these opportunities require that you do the learning and sometimes the opportunities require that you primarily be involved in the teaching, coaching, and/or mentoring. Either way, the goal is to learn, progress, and move forward as you attempt to be better equipped in your philanthropic leadership.

WORKSHOPS

In Winter Park, Florida, Rollins College offers learning opportunities at their Philanthropy and Nonprofit Leadership Center. Here they offer workshops and training relating to everything from organizing your philanthropy to running your board. What is important is that schools, like Rollins, give both donors and executive directors of charities opportunities to learn specific tools, wisdom, and knowledge to become better philanthropic leaders. It also allows these individuals to get to know each other, share their stories, and expand their network of learning and working together as they serve within their community. More and more universities, community colleges, and private graduate schools offer similar courses like the ones at Rollins. As a philanthropic leader, you should enroll in a workshop or training session where you can refine your skills, learn new insights, and grow as a leader.

If there is not an organization in your community that offers this type of workshop, then you may need to travel to annual events hosted by such organizations as Generous Giving or the Association of Small Foundations. Both of these groups offer workshops, seminars, and forums where you can learn to improve your work as a philanthropic leader. Likewise, you or your foundation may want to host your own workshops for friends and like-minded donors. This will take more leadership to host your own events, but you may find it to be one of the greatest gifts you give others. You may want to start by having a trusted attorney who is skilled in nonprofit law to speak on board compliance issues or you may simply want to share your own stories of what it means to be a philanthropic leader. Either way, as you create learning opportunities, you will continue to grow with others.

DIALOGUE WITH DONORS

Another opportunity for learning to occur is through strategic donor dialogue events. Rollins College (same as above) hosts events for donors to share their thoughts, feelings, and strategies for effective philanthropy. You may have such an opportunity in your own community to attend and participate in. A "dialogue with donors" event is an opportunity where community leaders, business leaders and other philanthropic leaders come together to learn about the work of philanthropy. Sometimes these events are luncheons offering fellowship and networking centered around a particular theme, the ethics of giving for example. Or other times these events occur at a donor's house where like-minded individuals come together to celebrate the joys of giving while discussing the best practices for avoiding donor fatigue. From corporate philanthropy initiatives to spirituality in philanthropy all participants have a voice for expression and learning in a friendly symposium.

If your community does not offer such events, or if they are not open for you to attend, then you may want to host one yourself from your own foundation. The point is to create learning opportunities, in safe environments, where others join you along the journey to learn and grow together. Donor dialogue events do not need to be elaborate. You may simply want to invite a fellow philanthropic leader for lunch to begin the conversation. Or you may want to gather on a regular basis for coffee and philanthropic dialogue. It is important that you start the dialogue for improving your world. By engaging donors in strategic dialogue, everyone will benefit.

CONNECTING NEEDS WITH DESIRES

Several years ago, my wife initiated a luncheon event where she invited needy charities to connect with big donors, private family foundations, and other philanthropic leaders. At these luncheons, a representative from each charity received about five minutes to present a brief overview of their work, mission, and needs. The donors, family foundations, and philanthropic leaders who were present had the opportunity to listen and learn about the different charities. After lunch and the presentations, different donors had the opportunity to initiate further any relationship they found desirous. Charity luncheons hosted by philanthropists begin new relationships and partnerships between donors and charities. This forum ultimately connects those who are needy with those who have the desire to give. You may have found that many times you do not know who needs your help. This forum connects both the donor and the charity in a way that is non-threatening, while allowing multiple charities to learn about each other and many donors to learn about them as well. Connecting needs with desires through luncheons is something you may choose to do as a philanthropic leader.

TAKE A TRIP

Many large, international nonprofit organizations allow their major donors to go on vision trips to see the work and progress of their charity. These trips include going all over the world from Southeast Asia, India, Africa, to the Dominican Republic to Central and South America. From participating in medical missions, building clean water wells, educating orphans, to equipping women with the tools to create dresses and clothes, these vision trips are great opportunities to learn more about the organizations you support as a philanthropic leader. Not only do you get to learn in greater detail about the particular work of the organization, but also you typically will travel along with other philanthropic leaders from around the country. The relationships you develop on these trips often continue long after the trip is over, while providing a journey of learning.

As your relationship with these international nonprofit organizations deepen, you will have opportunities to go beyond a passive observer on a vision trip to an active participant who takes a particular trip to instill your own expertise, knowledge, and wisdom as a co-learner to their employees. One particular friend of mine, Tom, travels each year to Istanbul to speak to a group of business people on behalf of a particular mission. He pays his own expenses and provides free counsel and wisdom to people who would otherwise not be able to afford to attend such a learning seminar. This type of initiative allows Tom to give of himself in a meaningful and significant way. His ability to pay his own way while teaching business concepts reaches far beyond simply donating dollars.

Another friend of mine demonstrates philanthropic leadership by going to Africa for a month or more each year to teach theology. Rather than simply writing a check to send missionaries or seminary professors overseas to live long-term and support their lifework, he donates his own time, money, and knowledge. Over many years, he has been able to develop authentic relationships with many Africans, learning their culture, their ways of thinking, and their ways of worshiping God. This reciprocal learning experience is what philanthropic leadership does at its best.

Your leadership will continue to grow and develop as you engage the lives of others in a meaningful way centered on reciprocal learning. Others will benefit from your initiative to seize and create learning opportunities, and you may find yourself surprised at how little you know and how much there is to learn. The great joy of the journey of learning is designed in such a way that you experience moments of liberating illumination where celebration is required.

LEADERSHIP EXERCISE

1. Who could begin to coach or mentor you this month on your philanthropic leadership journey?
2. What is the most significant thing you have learned so far from reading this book?
3. Describe one of the best learning experiences you have had as a philanthropic leader.
4. What one class, workshop, or seminar do you need to attend to grow as a leader?
5. Reflect upon a time in your life when the paradox of learning occurred. Who did you teach and how did they end up teaching you?

LIBERATING—CELEBRATING THE FRUIT

*But we had to celebrate and be glad, because this brother of
yours was dead and is alive again; he was lost and is found.*
—Luke 15:32

There is nothing quite like a great party! Celebrating accomplishments, goals achieved, and problems solved, brings satisfaction as you get to enjoy the fruit of your labor. When you reach different levels of success, you need to celebrate those milestones. A milestone not only serves as a reminder of how far you have reached, but also it serves as a reminder of where you have come from and where you are going. Celebrating the fruit of your philanthropic initiatives gives an opportunity for everyone on your team to feel appreciated. This is when you honor your team for the work they have participated in.

Throwing a party may be one of the most significant things you do as a philanthropic leader. Your team will enjoy the fruit of their labor in an environment where joy, love and peace are celebrated. Your celebration may include an awards ceremony, highlighting specific individuals and their work of philanthropy.

Or it may include awarding the successes of team projects and specific highlights that occurred over the course of the initiative. I recently returned from a celebration in Buenos Aries, Argentina where different social entrepreneurs were honored for outstanding work in philanthropic initiatives with the poor in rural parts of Argentina. This event took place as a partnership between the United Bank of Switzerland's (UBS) global philanthropic services and the Ashoka organization (www.ashoka.org). These organizations encourage social entrepreneurs to become change-makers who in turn make a significant difference in the lives of others. The celebration honored philanthropic initiatives like bringing solar powered panels to huts and small rural businesses where many people experienced having a light bulb for the first time in their lives. This one project brought light to homes and businesses, and new light to hearts where hope is beginning to shine. This is the liberation that arrives when philanthropic leaders bring hope and empowerment to those they serve. When this occurs, you need to rejoice and celebrate.

When you bring about liberation to the poor, the hungry, and the homeless, when you help the widow, the orphan, and the fatherless, when you educate a child or reduce adult illiteracy, you enlighten another human to a whole new world of hope, life, and love. When that occurs you know you are on the journey of celebrating the fruit of your philanthropic work. A simple smile, a warm hug, and thunderous applause are all ways you can empower another person, restore dignity, and continue a future of goodness within humanity. Sometimes celebrating accomplishments is as simple as a smile and a hug, yet celebrating the heart is powerful. Sometimes offering a word of affirmation and recognition to an individual restores respect, hope, and a powerful sense of significance in their life. These acts of celebrating are free gifts from the heart to the heart of another fellow human. This is where loving humankind, (i.e., your philanthropy), truly counts.

Another way you may choose to celebrate a job well done or a specific individual is by granting more money to that particular individual or project. When this is clearly portrayed in front of others, then the message you send communicates that where great performance occurs, these individuals and programs will be reinforced. Sometimes this entails making a program stronger or giving a certain leader more tools and education to further his or her own development. Other times, this may call for reproducing a certain philanthropic project in other places of the world. When a particular project succeeds with flying colors, then these are the ones that need celebrating and reproducing.

The Rafiki Foundation is a charity that works to provide safety and healthcare to orphaned and vulnerable children while providing the education necessary to help them become godly contributors to their communities. Once Rafiki gained success with their orphanage centers in Africa, they were able to celebrate the successes by implementing more centers in more countries. Reinforcing and reproducing positive results is especially vital when you leverage your resources in such a way that it does not jeopardize your overall operations.

> ## LIFE PRINCIPLE: CELEBRATE OTHERS IN A WAY THAT HONORS THEM

Knowing how to celebrate the successes of philanthropic leaders is just as important, if not more important, than simply celebrating them. Knowing the people within your organization makes a difference. When charities invite me to be honored for my philanthropic work, the last thing I want to receive is a plaque to hang on my wall or a trophy to stick somewhere. For me, I find this type of recognition a waste of my donated dollars and a waste of the charity's time. For others, receiving that plaque gives them a sense of pride and accomplishment. When properly displayed in one's office or home, it serves as both a reminder of their philanthropic work and as a conversation starter with others. Thus, you need to understand the importance of celebrating certain donors and/or philanthropic leaders in this way. However, some donors and/or philanthropic leaders prefer to simply spend quality time with executive directors and other staff. For this type of individual, this is a great reward. I am honored every time the founder and president of International Justice Mission stays in my home when he comes to visit Orlando. For me, it is a real treat to provide a free place for him to stay while enjoying his company and fellowship. Even though this type of honor does not come in the spotlight, it is felt just as much as being celebrated in front of large crowds. Thus, it is very important to know what makes people feel important, celebrated, and honored. For some, it is a simple thank you letter while for others it is a nice plaque. The important thing is that philanthropic leadership honors people and their successes in a way that they want to be honored.

A few years ago, I had the privilege of being invited to go on an all-guys fishing trip in Canada north of Vancouver. Only five men from across the country were chosen to be a part of this trip. There were two others who represented the charitable organization that was hosting the trip. This small fellowship of people that came together to retreat and enjoy the outdoors was actually a form of honoring the organization's philanthropic leaders, while building relationships with a few select others. Even though this private fishing trip may not have appeared much like a celebration, it was. The fishing trip served several purposes for the organization. First, it was part of their ten-year anniversary celebration of being in operation. The president and CEO spoke of past successes, while sharing the vision for the future. The trip also allowed for philanthropic leaders to share their own stories and reasons why they appreciate the work of this particular charity. This gave everyone present an opportunity to share their personal story of what this organization means to them. Thus, it engaged everyone's participation and perspective and it honored the few who were selected to be there. This type of thank you retreat was truly a treat and celebration.

Another unique and beneficial way to celebrate your charity of choice is to throw a party on behalf of the charity. My wife and I served with two other couples to host a party for the Rafiki Foundation (www.rafiki-foundation.org). Rafiki was in the process of moving its headquarters from San Antonio, Texas to the Central Florida region. After several meetings to iron out event details, we decided to invest our time, resources, and energy to honor the arrival and work of this group. We invited a large crowd of friends, community leaders, pastors, and other people who we thought would be interested in learning more about Rafiki. And to ensure that this event would not be a fundraiser, or that anyone would be pressured to give, we made it a celebration party where people were invited to simply have fun, fellowship, and get to know the organization. The event did not cost Rafiki a dime and no one felt pressured to make a donation. Rather, the small group of couples lead the way as philanthropic leaders by communicating their excitement and passion for Rafiki's arrival to town.

Although celebrations come in many different forms, it is important to realize and understand the power of celebrating true successes. When you reach a pinnacle of success as a philanthropic leader, you should celebrate. Celebrating success energizes everyone involved and refuels excitement and inspiration. Philanthropic leaders understand the importance of liberation from bondage of poverty, sex slavery, oppression and all other forms of human suffering. When liberation occurs, you must celebrate the fruit of your labor. It may simply entail celebrating life to the fullest when your loved one overcomes cancer or when you educate an adult on how to read. Wherever and whatever form of liberation from bondage and breakthroughs occur, a celebration honors people and creates an environment that sustains the human spirit.

LEADERSHIP EXERCISE

1. What philanthropic accomplishment, goal, or milestone do you need to celebrate?
2. Who in your foundation or charity needs special recognition for a job well done? How would this particular individual like to be honored?
3. What particular social project exceeded your expectations? Who was the driving force behind it? How can you celebrate this person's success?
4. Make a list of the top three public charities in your community that you would like to highlight and celebrate by hosting a party in their honor. Who needs to be invited to make this a special occasion? What awards need to be given?
5. At your first philanthropic party, begin a pictorial journal of the event. By creating a photo album of past successes, you create a historicity of your foundation's successes. You may even want to document the event on video to share with other participants within your organization.

Living—Leading a Legacy

To state the facts frankly is not to despair the future nor indict the past. The prudent heir takes careful inventory of his legacies and gives a faithful accounting to those whom he owes an obligation of trust.
—John F. Kennedy

People measure one's legacy by both how they lived and what they left behind. From the values they instilled to their children to the museums, schools, and hospitals they built with their philanthropic giving, one's legacy continues on. The role of philanthropy is important to your legacy. Anyone can will his or her fortune to different projects, purposes, and people, but it takes leadership to lead your legacy into the future. Rather than thinking your legacy is something you leave behind, begin to think of your legacy as something you lead now. By leading your legacy now, you will ensure that the next generation of philanthropic leaders will have the tools, values, beliefs, and knowledge that come from actively living what you believe. In other words, do not wait until you die to give your valuables away. It is next to impossible to will away values, beliefs, and life wisdom without relating to others now. Yes, you can leave money behind, but the values that go with how to handle the money are more important than the money itself.

Practicing What You Preach

When you practice what you preach, your behavior and words come into alignment as you live your daily life. It is important as a philanthropic leader to speak the truth in love whether it is positive or negative. This type of honesty takes a good dose of humility. As you live out your passion for philanthropy in relationship with others, it is important that your actions and words, your beliefs and values, your ethics and responsibilities continue to be lived with integrity. Ultimately, who you are as a leader is more important than any temporal amount of money you give. It is good to watch *It's a Wonderful Life* during the holidays. This movie, staring Donna Reed and Jimmy Stewart, shares the story of George Bailey (played by Stewart) who arrives at a crossroad in life and must choose between being a man of his word, or being like Mr. Potter, a man who cares only for himself. The movie reveals what the town of Bedford Falls would be like if George Bailey had not lived. Without his compassion and care for others, without his self-sacrificing way of life, without his attempt to instill dignity and hope to those he helped through his building and loan business, Bedford Falls would have been radically different. Bailey made a difference by living with integrity, by practicing philanthropic leadership and by his love for humankind. He practiced what he preached even as he underwent deep soul anguish as he searched for meaning and hope in life.

Likewise, practicing what you preach is not always easy. These are the battlegrounds where you, as a leader, reveal what you truly believe. This is also the place where some of your greatest learning will occur. By fulfilling your promises and pledges to give, even when things have gone terribly wrong (be it in the economy or with a particular charitable cause), the crucible of living as a person of your word refines your leadership character. You may learn to be slower to make a financial pledge over a period of several years or you may learn to put certain giving stipulations as you progress with a particular charity. Nevertheless, when you are known for keeping your commitments, even when things do not occur as you would have liked, the character you model may be worth more than any financial gift.

MENTORING

If you have faced the crucibles of leadership and have survived, then you are a likely fit to be a good mentor. This does not mean that you will be perfect or that you will pass every test life throws your way with flying colors; it does mean that you know how to walk down the paths of adversity and continue on. Being able to continue on in the face of adversity is a large part of what it means to be a philanthropic leader. Whether you are attempting to reduce world hunger, or increase involvement in your local parent-teacher association (PTA) participation, living forward in a mentoring relationship could be one of the greatest relationships you experience as a philanthropic leader. By going through life with a younger person who you mentor and with whom you remain transparent, you will not only begin to have a dear friend, but you will also be able to lead your legacy now.

High schools across America typically hold a career day or career week each year where you can speak and share what it means to be doctor, lawyer, architect, etc. As a philanthropic leader, these events are great places to discover a new relationship with a young person who desires to make a difference. Even though the young person may want to be a doctor or a lawyer when he or she grows older, you have the ability to instill in him or her now the values of being a philanthropic leader. By working together on community volunteer projects, the time is now to instill a lifestyle of philanthropy in the next generation.

You may have a program in your community that works with troubled teenagers who also need mentoring. Many young boys who do not have a father or a positive father figure in their life could use someone like you to mentor and model healthy relating. If you work with one young person in high school, college, or a recent graduate and show him or her how they can experience the joys and blessings of living for others, you will begin to lead your legacy.

LEAD AT HOME

You may also begin to model a life of philanthropy in your home with your children. Take them to a homeless shelter to serve food. Have your family go on an inner city mission trip to be a warm loving presence to children who may not come from the best of homes. You can begin an art class or a game of pick-up basketball. You can start a meals-on-wheels program for your local church, synagogue, or mosque. It may simply mean inviting those who have no family during Thanksgiving to join your family for a good hearty meal and a pleasant conversation; it may be someone you work with, or someone you know who is lonely. The point is to start as early as you can with your children to model and mentor how they can make a difference by simply engaging another person. A warm smile, a gentle hug, a kind word of appreciation, or a heartfelt prayer demonstrates the kindness that marks your life. These acts, of course, do not require money, but they are a return to the basics of what it means to be human: not turning away when you see your neighbor in distress, but turning to them to help, to love, and to serve.

LEADERSHIP EXERCISE

1. How has the paradigm of leading a legacy rather than leaving a legacy impacted your thinking?
2. Have you been quick to make a promise only to regret it later on? If so, what did you do? What did you learn?
3. Who could you begin a mentoring relationship with as you enter a relationship to lead a legacy? Describe what you would desire this relationship to evolve into.
4. What have you learned from a young person about philanthropic leadership?
5. What philanthropic experiences can you lead your family to experience that build the values and beliefs of what it means to be a philanthropic leader?

CHAPTER FOUR:
WISDOM

How much better to get wisdom than gold, to
choose understanding rather than silver!
—Proverbs 16:16

WISDOM, LIKE LOVE, IS A precious gift that once given, increases in the giver. This is why wisdom is better than gold and understanding greater than silver. When you give your money away, it is gone. When you give wisdom away, you retain it as it helps others. Becoming a wise philanthropic leader is one of the greatest goals before you. This is a lifelong journey of learning and maturing as a leader. You may have learned wisdom from your grandparents, parents, a neighbor or a friend, but you must continue to seek wisdom and practice it with your daily choices. When you listen to wisdom, and commit to leading by it, you will not be disappointed.

BUFFETT'S WISDOM

It takes twenty years to build a reputation and five minutes to ruin it.
If you think about that, you'll do things differently.
—Warren Buffett

If anyone knows what it means to be rich, it is Warren Buffett. As one of the wealthiest persons who has ever lived, he knows about money. He knows how to make it and he knows how to invest it. He knows how to save it and he knows how to compound it. However, Mr. Buffett has never been too fond of spending it. And maybe that is his secret to success. But, on June 26, 2006, he shocked the world by giving one of the biggest warnings to the rich in recent history. In a nutshell, the warning did not come as rebuke, a cautious eye, or even a declaration of "watch out." No, Mr. Buffett gave a warning to the rich without even giving a warning by the way in which he gave his money. It is vital to see the wisdom he applied with his philanthropy. To illustrate, Alice Schroeder writes:

> The man who was, at the time, the second richest person on earth was giving away his money without leaving a trace of himself behind. He had spent all his life rolling up the snowball as if it were an extension of himself; yet he would establish no Warren Buffett Foundation, no Buffett hospital wing, no college or university endowment or building with his name on it. To donate the money without naming something after himself, without controlling personally how it would be spent—to put the money in the coffers of another foundation that he had selected for its competence and efficiency, rather than creating a whole new empire—upended every convention of giving. No major donor had ever done such a thing before.
>
> That Warren Buffett had done this was both surprising and predictable. An unconventional thinker and problem-solver, he was making a gesture against philanthropic waste and grandiosity. The Gates Foundation got its

money, but had to spend each installment—and fast. The decision was unusual, highly personal, a form of teaching by example, and—naturally—enormously attention-getting. Meanwhile, in another sense, this was a classic Buffett no-lose deal. He had stunned the world by giving away almost all of his money by earmarking it, yet got to keep most of it until he actually transferred the shares.[38]

It's Not About You

There are several important warnings for the rich embedded within Mr. Buffett's wisdom. First, it is not about you. Buffett's decision to give was not about enamoring himself with the public now or in the years to come. The second warning concerns all of the possible problems that foundations face with large sums of money. Because money is enticing to those who want it, attempting to lead and manage a large foundation long term often becomes a jockeying board for power, position, and prestige. And when the money continues to sit, lawsuits often arise over everything from board control to exercising fiduciary responsibility. In other words, many large foundations bring problems. The third warning Buffett gave to the rich is to be wise about how you give your money. In this particular case, Buffett did not want to personally get involved in the daily details of strategically giving money. Nevertheless, he understands the importance of knowing another trusted, wise, and intelligent individual whom would not be tempted to take his share of the cash, but rather do the work of a philanthropic leader. In this case, Bill Gates is the man who Buffett trusts.

By entrusting his money to a friend who has more money than he, Buffett created another layer of safety. In addition, Buffett cut out possible family feuds among siblings and other relatives. Finally, Buffett gives one of the loudest warnings to the rich by having predetermined limits on how long the foundation can hold onto his money. By law, any foundation is required to only give five percent of its assets away yearly. There is no set legal requirement for how much one may take in personal salary from those assets. So, if Buffett gives tens of billions away and the Gates Foundation, receiving it, has no instructions, then the door is open for many people to line their pockets with personal salaries and fees (e.g. attorneys and accountants feeing the funds, board members and directors enjoying nice benefits and large salaries). In this instance, funding directives create another layer of stewardship. Hence, the Gates Foundation must give Buffett's money away wisely and quickly without inviting the many evils that come from pride and greed.

START SMALL

It does not matter if you have 1 million dollars, 100 million, or billions like Buffett to give away. The sum does not matter. What matters is that you start small. Starting small gives you the opportunity to test faithfulness. As the old saying goes, when you are faithful in the small things, then you can graduate to the bigger things.[8] Too often, donors get caught up in the emotions and excitement of helping another, and give too much too soon. As a result, they see how their hard-earned funding went to wasteful spending. A friend of mine got caught in the trap of starting too big too soon, and he had to backpedal. The only problem is that backpedaling does not work. Once your money is given, it is gone. Once your time is spent, you can never recapture it. And backpedaling often leaves regret and hurt relationships, for it usually signifies that something went wrong. Nevertheless, starting small means you start with wisdom.

Wisdom says it is smart to start your philanthropic giving on a small scale. By doing this, you are able to measure your giving results. Is your time being spent wisely? Is your money being spent and invested wisely? Are your relationships healthy? Do the charities you work with respect you as a philanthropic leader, or do they only see you as a bank? As you start small, questions like these bring clarity to your giving. If you start off giving too much too soon, then others may see you as a threat. Or they may be blindsided by the amount of money you have given, and think you will continue to give in large amounts in the future. Or, like my friend, you will have given your gift while believing the organization would handle your gift one way, and only when it is too late, realize that the organization

---

8 See Matthew 25:21.

either mishandled your grant or they were simply not in the position to adequately manage it.

What seems like a small price to you may be an overwhelming sum to a nonprofit charity. Wisdom says it is good to ask as many questions as possible, for only in asking questions do you learn. For example, it is wise to ask, "What do you consider a major donor?" or, "What is the largest amount of money your organization has received? Did it come from an individual or did a foundation give it as a grant?" You may even want to see a breakdown of the recipient's proposed budget. If an organization is asking you for money, then you have every right to ask questions and to see their strategic plan, budget, and key people who will execute their proposal with your funding. Another wise question that I always ask start-up nonprofits and other charities in regard to start-up programs is the following: Will it fly?

BUT WILL IT FLY?

When I was fourteen years old, I received a letter from a friend, entitled, "But Will It Fly?" The title of the letter speaks volumes to philanthropic leadership. As I speak with people on a regular basis who want advice about starting a nonprofit organization, and who also want funding, I will often ask them, "But will it fly?" For too long, great people with gigantic hearts want to do even bigger things for others, and often they want to do it in the name of God. I have nothing against doing things for the glory of God, but the problem is, many of these individuals are not only unknowledgeable about running a 501 (c) 3, but they also rarely have sufficient funding or advice. When this is compounded with the underlying assumption, "if I believe God enough, and pray really hard, then I'll be rich like these other people I know," then I have to tell these individuals that just because the Lord has blessed one person's ministry does not mean that you too will become the next celebrity pastor or charity. When there are over 2 million nonprofits in America today, it is easy to think that anyone can start and run one. And the temptation is to model your philanthropic 501 (c) 3 after the next multi-million dollar nonprofit, in hopes that you too will become a major voice in America. Like winning the lottery, this wishful thinking typically puts major stress and pressure on individuals as they hope to become the next major player.

Literally thousands of nonprofits established in recent years in America should have been for-profit companies. But because they are either somewhat religious or social in concept, the people behind these organizations believed it is wrong to make a buck providing these types of needs. At the end of the day, these same individuals come begging for money in order to survive. Yet, if these same groups would have established for-profit entities, then they would either generate enough cash for staying power, or they would fold. In other words, if a for-profit company cannot fly, it folds. But rarely in the nonprofit world will you see struggling nonprofit organizations fold when they cannot make it. Rather you will get hit up with giving more and more money, like pouring cash down a bottomless pit. It never seems to be enough.

No matter how much money you have given as a philanthropic leader, you may need to step up and provide either wisdom and strategies to revamp the organization to make it more effective and efficient or you may need to call it quits. There is nothing wrong with folding an organization if it does not fly. In many cases, this frees up individuals to work in other sectors where they can truly prosper and succeed. Everyone is not meant or called to work in the nonprofit world no matter how appealing it may seem.

After giving a presentation on philanthropic leadership, a gentlemen wanted to run a few ideas by me about a nonprofit that he hoped to establish. After listening to his idea, it occurred to me that his idea would most likely fly high as a for-profit company. The main reason he wanted his concept to be nonprofit, was that he did not want to risk his money or investors' money. He believed, like many, that the nonprofit world is a quick way to generate cash, because people are ready to give and want to receive a tax deduction. Even though it is true that most people are somewhat generous, and they want their tax deductions, the nonprofit world has fallen prey to pitiful strategies and individuals who only see a quick way to generate money for some good cause. The good cause in many cases is providing themselves with income by asking wealthy donors for money. So once again, I ask, "But will it fly?"

I received a request to grant approximately $600,000 to a nonprofit organization that wanted to print thousands of books to give to our troops serving in Iraq. This is a classic example of an individual who probably believed he could make a better salary as a nonprofit author than a for-profit one. Rather than seeing if his book would fly on the open market, he had rich friends fund the printing and free distribution of his books. Economist William Easterly speaks directly to this concept of philanthropic leadership. The market place is capable of testing ideas to see if they will fly. For example, the Harry Potter book flew off the shelves and into the hands of millions of children, not because the author wanted to make children smile, but because she wanted to meet a need. Children liked the stories and wanted more of them. Likewise, when we meet real needs based not on our assumptions as philanthropic leaders, or what we believe the needs of the poor are, but rather on what the poor tell us they need, then we can provide solutions to the very things the poor are seeking. By shifting the focus from our perspective to theirs, new wisdom and insight on true needs is gained.

Closed for Ministry

You can have sleek brochures, a celebrity board of directors and advisors, the greatest network and name power, and still be closed for ministry. A dear friend of mine had it all, or at least it appeared that way from the surface. From US Open champions to Grammy Award Winning singers, congressmen to celebrity pastors, this start-up ministry had all of the endorsements money cannot buy, and yet it was not enough. The start-up 501 (c) 3 lasted less than five years. There were many indicators of why it closed. The never-ending need to ask people for money and the many administrative costs of running a nonprofit, combined with other concerns, all contributed to the decision to shut it down. But the need for leadership, both personal and corporate, appeared lacking from the beginning, when the nonprofit was in the initial idea stage.

| LIFE PRINCIPLE: IT TAKES WISDOM TO RECOGNIZE |
| FAILURE AND COURAGE TO ADMIT IT |

Many people who find themselves in the wanderlust of thinking about how great it would be to start their own nonprofit should be very slow to start before simply jumping in. Although these individuals know a handful of wealthy givers, they do not understand how their relationship changes once they ask their friends for money. And since many of these individuals have never raised any significant amount of money year after year, they do not understand the extreme burdens of constantly raising money. I try to encourage many of these individuals to see if they can do what they want to do in the for-profit marketplace. If the for-profit marketplace will support it, they don't need to raise funds from the nonprofit sector. Wisdom continues to show how these people would prefer to lose your money in a failed nonprofit, rather than pay back a bank loan. When faced with people who are looking to start a nonprofit, it takes wisdom to recognize what is going on and courage to address it in a healthy way.

A BEGGAR AND A SANDWICH

I happened to be in downtown Orlando, where many of the homeless hang out, on a Saturday afternoon with my wife. We were walking to lunch at a local sandwich café when a local beggar approached us for money so he could eat. We told the gentleman we would be more than happy for him to come in and dine with us; we would pay for his meal rather than simply give him money. The homeless gentleman declined our offer. Other times, with other individuals, I have had the privilege of eating with homeless people and getting to know their individual stories, their hearts, and their lives. But what emerged this afternoon was completely different. The café manager saw what had occurred, and he began to share with us about the activity among the homeless around his restaurant.

"I know all of these guys around here, and you should not give them any money. They're not hungry. All they want is the cash, to buy booze and drugs. I had one fine gentleman in here one day who actually bought this homeless man a sandwich, chips and a drink, and once the generous patron had finished his meal and was gone, what do you know, the homeless man came back inside to try to sell me his sandwich back. They don't want to eat in here; they just want your money. And anyway, there are many shelters and soup kitchens down here, but they refuse to go there, because those places have rules," he said.

When these types of occurrences happen, if you feel generous, safe, and have the time, then test the situation. Start small, use wisdom, and do not flash your ability to give where it may not be safe or appropriate. Sometimes the homeless beggar truly is hungry and is willing to share some of their heart with you. And when this occurs, great things can happen.

BE WISE IN ALL SITUATIONS

It was late at night when a friend and I were driving home from an out of town NHL game in Tampa. We pulled into a gas station to refuel off of some remote exit. As soon as we jumped out of our car, we were approached by a couple who asked for money to stay another night in the little run down motel across the street. Here, again, what am I going to do? Do I simply give them the cash that they are requesting? Do I turn away from my own humanity and lie to them, "Sorry man, I don't have any cash?" or do I probe their story, and get more entrenched? It was late, and I needed to be wise. Revealing the cash in my wallet was not a wise thing to do. So, once the gas tank was filled (paid for with a credit card), I suggested that the couple meet me across the street inside the lobby of the local motel where I would personally see if they were actually staying there and how much money they owed the motel for another night's rest. With all of this attention to detail, they were quick to say "Never mind, we don't want you to go to all of that trouble." "It is no trouble at all," I replied. "I will drive across the street and help you stay at the motel." Unfortunately, the couple really did not want a night's rest at the motel, and wisdom unveiled their intentions. By starting small in conversation and probing deeper, I exercised wisdom while being available to truly help.

Policies and Procedures

One helpful way to implement giving by starting small, and using wisdom, is to create your own giving policies and procedures for both personal contributions and giving from your foundation. This may entail that you never give more than $10,000 initially to a new organization to see how well it responds and uses your gift, or it may entail not giving to an organization that does not allow you to see their budget, strategic plan, and personally be involved in other ways, besides financially. You may decide to never give to the homeless directly on a street corner, but rather point them to a specific soup kitchen and/or shelter you support. From choosing not to give to friends, because once money is mixed with friends things can prove unfavorable for you and your relationship, simply tell your friends that you have found it wise to cherish their relationship more than getting commingled in their charity or cause. Or you may need to create a ninety-day waiting period for any organization appearing desperate for money. This is one such policy my wife and I share, simply because organizations that cannot wait for money, most likely are not running their organization in a wise way. And we have found that our money tends to go to pay off bad debt rather than make a real difference. Some groups need to learn wisdom and the wisdom of starting small. Not meeting their immediate demands is one way to help them understand all that they can accomplish without money. By establishing specific policies and procedures, you will lead with wisdom.

Your Mission

Every philanthropic leader needs a mission and vision statement. Your mission is vital to your success as a leader because it gives you clarity and focus and defines what you are about. Your mission should start small. Too many organizations try to do everything and end up failing because of the inability to focus on one single issue, problem, or cause. By starting small, you can set manageable goals to reach, targets to hit, and problems to solve. And with each achievement you celebrate, you may eventually reevaluate and progress to expand your mission and scope of philanthropic initiative. However, it is wise to start small with your mission and vision statement.

Your mission statement defines who you are and what you are about, while your vision statement casts a picture of what you want to achieve. Your vision statement clearly defines what you hope to achieve. Some of the best mission and vision statements are short, simple, and to the point. In one or two sentences, at most, you should be able to clearly share your mission and vision.

Leadership Exercise

In this exercise, first answer the questions below. Next, create both a personal and foundational policy and procedure guideline to giving wisely. Then if you do not already have a mission and vision statement, begin to work on one. Remember it should be simple, clear, and concise. You may want to have a public statement you give to those who inquire about your foundation and you may also want to have a private statement for you and your employees. This allows you to have a working operational mission statement internally, and an external one for public relations, elevator encounters, and those seeking grants.

1. Make a list of wisdom principles you live by.
2. From your list of wisdom principles, choose your top three and describe how each one of those has impacted your success as a leader.
3. Think of a time when you did not practice wisdom in charitable giving. What happened? How did it make you feel afterwards?
4. Have you ever made the mistake of giving too much too soon? If so, describe what happened.
5. What other life story comes to mind, an encounter where you have been asked to give, on the spot, to a homeless person? What did you do? Did you act with love and with wisdom? How?

COMMON SENSE AND DISCERNMENT

Common sense is genius dressed in its working clothes.
—Ralph Waldo Emerson

Voltaire's words, "Common sense is not so common," continue to hold true today. Within the world of philanthropy, finding common sense is like finding a rare and precious jewel. It is hard to find, but when you do, it is a beautiful thing to behold. The basic underlying assumption is that other people—charities—know how to handle your money better than you do. And this is common sense to those who want your money. But often it is the wealthy businessperson, who understands far better than those who run nonprofits, how to maximize resources, minimize expenses, and make a difference, while generating a surplus. And this is not as hard as it may appear if you use common sense.

EVERYONE WANTS YOUR MONEY

But it is not just the development directors, fundraising gurus, and community foundations that act as if they know what is best for you and your assets. Often your law firm, accounting firm, or financial firm also wants you to believe that they know best how you should contribute to others. Whether it is setting up a private foundation or overseeing your charitable activities, these experts know what is best. Or at least this seems to make sense, does it not? These firms and experts do have all of the fancy initials behind their names and they are qualified to direct you on how you should give, so it only makes sense that you should trust these people to set up your charitable gift annuity or pool your resources into a charitable mutual fund. It does make sense to take out that second mortgage or strategically give a portion of your life insurance to your favorite charity. And if you do not have a favorite charity, then no worries, these experts know how to maximize your charitable giving, while ensuring any surplus goes to their charity of choice. You should not be surprised when they want you to give them your money now, so that they can take a portion of it and give it back to you for the remainder of your life. Doesn't this make sense? Isn't this wonderful?

Unfortunately, even though there is great pressure to conform to the advice, recommendation, and input from the experts, the best common sense is yours, not theirs. But this life lesson usually comes too late if you are not actively practicing discernment. In other words, you need to beware of even the best advice from your most trusted advisor, because many of these experts and firms have everything from hidden fees to their own personal agenda and biases that reach far beyond what you might ever think or imagine. That is not to say that all lawyers, accountants, certified financial planners, and nonprofit consultants are villains. On the contrary, they appear to truly want to help, and many of them, especially the religious financial advisors "do all things for God's glory." Never mind the many Biblical warnings against those who appear godly, but are really after your money. Never mind that your common sense does not align with theirs. But this is how so many good philanthropic people get used. Many financial tools and tricks are complicated and confusing, especially in regard to the ever-changing tax code, so you feel it is best to defer to their judgment.

Yet something deep inside your gut, your common sense, tells you that these ideas and concepts just do not ring true. You should not take out a second mortgage. You should not become a generous giver to the point where you become needy. You should not give in order for the charity of your choice to pay you some small amount of money for the remainder of your life. What if they are no longer around? What if there is fraud? Your gut may tell you something is not right, but you cannot quite put your finger on it. Maybe you ask a friend, or get a second or third opinion. And maybe everyone continues to sing the same song and give you the same mantra. Philanthropic leaders challenge the status quo. You should seek advice from your attorneys, accountants, financial planners, and other advisors, but you need to check their advice with your common sense and discernment. Ask clarifying questions about timetables, fees, and how they will truly bring value to your philanthropic initiatives. As you learn to ask strategic questions, listen for alignment and look for loopholes in their answers. Look at the larger context of their personal lives and see if they practice what they preach with their own money.

WANTS VERSUS NEEDS

The majority of nonprofits want your money, but they need your leadership even more. Money will only last so long, but the leadership you give can continue on. There will be a point in your philanthropic leadership where money must be kept and leadership given. It is in these tense moments where the long-term *need* must trump the short-term *want*. It is here where London's professors of leadership, Rob Goffee and Gareth Jones, illustrate that leaders are "to give people what they need rather than what they want. They communicate a tough empathy that balances respect for the individual, the task at hand, and, ultimately, the higher purpose."[39]

The philanthropic leader uses discernment to know when money is only a temporary band-aid that may bring a smile, but it truly does not fix the underlying issues at hand. This is where you discern the difference between the wants and needs of the organization you are serving. Too often leaders keep fanning the smoke rather than fighting the fire. When this occurs, no matter how much money you can throw at a problem, if you are only fanning the smoke, the fire remains. It takes discernment and common sense to know the difference. You must discern real needs from mere wants and lead accordingly.

LEADERSHIP PRACTICES INVENTORY: DISCERNING WHAT IS NEEDED

Although Jim Kouzes and Berry Posner's work does not entail philanthropic leadership, their "five practices of exemplary leadership" from *Leadership Practices Inventory*, acts as guiding principles for you to use: model the way, inspire a shared vision, challenge the process, enable others to act, and encourage the heart.[40] These five points portray the work of philanthropy.

MODEL THE WAY

Philanthropic leaders, who model the way, tend to give in order to promote more philanthropy. Clearly, Warren Buffett's $37 billion donation to the Bill and Melinda Gates Foundation models the way for the other 270 billionaires and over five million millionaires in America. But whether you are giving money, time, energy, or engaging in a mentoring relationship, you need to discern if your leadership is truly modeling the way for philanthropic leaders. Is your leadership worth following? Is your leadership worth modeling to others? By discerning your own behavior and the context from which you lead, you may want to perform an inventory on your leadership.

INSPIRE A SHARED VISION

Philanthropic leaders inspire a shared vision among world leaders, other philanthropists, and local recipients of benevolent investing. For example, the One organization continues to get government leaders from the White House to Parliament to forgive debt from developing nations. Rather than raising billions of dollars to funnel into philanthropic endeavors, One is currently spreading its vision to inspire young people all over the world to become aware of global poverty and the HIV/AIDS crisis. The question remains, how do you inspire a shared vision among those you serve? Is your vision only from your point-of-view or has it risen among the participants who serve along with you? Common sense continues to reveal that where the vision is shared, the team is internally motivated. If you discern that your vision is neither inspirational nor shared, then it may be time to reconsider the vision of your philanthropic initiatives with those who serve with you.

CHALLENGE THE PROCESS

MTV models how to challenge the process. Thanks to "the global revolution in cheap electronics, smart software and wireless mobility," MTV believes that by this year, 2010, 280 million Africans will have cellular service, which they intend to tap into.[41] On June 18, 2007, Quentin Hardy wrote an article entitled "Hope and Profit in Africa," which reveals how MTV desires to educate the poor on everything from micro-financing to AIDS prevention—while making a profit. As MTV challenges beliefs, worldviews, values, and capitalism, they are also challenging the way philanthropic investments occur. By going to the most remote parts of the globe, MTV believes it can build consumer markets while fighting AIDS in Africa. This type of philanthropic leadership is viewed as philanthropic capitalism, whereby the extreme poor actively participate in their economic development. Rather than MTV simply handing out cell phones and giving away free music, they realize that the extreme poor do, in fact, have money and they want to be actively engaged in their own economy, the same as humans do anywhere else on the planet.

Does your philanthropic leadership challenge the process of giving, living, and leading, or does it simply get lost in the status quo? How can you better challenge your own beliefs and thoughts in ways that make sense?

ENABLE OTHERS TO ACT

Philanthropy is ultimately about enabling others to act. MTV is not the only company modeling the way by challenging the process in Africa. Corporations like Google and Microsoft too are enabling others to act as well. Hardy continues in *Forbes*:

> Google is giving away writing and calendar software to schools and governments in Rwanda and Kenya and pressing countries to open up their Internet policies. The idea is to do good works—and build a customer base … In the face of this free competitor, Microsoft cut its prices for a bundle of Windows and other software to just $3 for users in poor countries worldwide, including most of Africa.[42]

This type of philanthropic investing enables others to act, because those you serve must be empowered to produce their own wealth. Keeping the extreme poor dependent upon handouts only perpetuates the problem and the cycle of poverty. As I toured the Drew Estates Factory in Nicaragua, I learned that this particular company not only employees people who would otherwise not have a job, but in addition, they pay them double the average salary in Nicaragua. By paying their people more, educating them with the necessary skills to work, and providing health care, this company is slowly lifting poverty through the selling of cigars. When your leadership enables the needy to act, you are on the path to producing wealth sustainability for the poor. When this takes place, hearts are encouraged.

ENCOURAGE THE HEART

Encouraging the heart produces a sense of satisfaction and gratitude in both the donor and recipient; both receive a blessing. However, by discerning when those you serve are emotionally down or discouraged, then it only makes sense to encourage their hearts. This synergy spurs you to look outward at others rather than inward at yourself. It keeps your philanthropic leadership focused on the people you serve and their emotional wellness and empowerment rather than on your agenda.

In summation, it only makes sense to use common sense and to actively discern what occurs around you. By acting on discernment and doing what makes sense, your leadership should prove fruitful. You need wisdom to discern between needs and wants, hidden agendas and motives, and the ability to lead in such a way that your followers are not only inspired to follow your leadership, but delighted to reach new grounds in their own personal development. As you model the way, inspire a vision that is truly shared, challenge the status quo, empower those around you, then you will have most likely already encouraged the hearts of those who serve alongside you.

LEADERSHIP EXERCISE

1. Is your leadership worth modeling? Why?
2. Is your vision solely yours or is it created from all of the participants with whom you lead? How is your philanthropic vision inspiring?
3. Are you able to think outside the box like MTV, by challenging the process of traditional philanthropic thought? If so, what are you doing that is radically different?
4. How does your philanthropic leadership enable those you serve to act? How does it empower them?
5. How do you encourage the hearts of those you serve? What would they say?

Measurements

Everything that can be counted does not necessarily count;
everything that counts cannot necessarily be counted.
—Albert Einstein

As a philanthropic leader, you must count the costs and measure the results. Measurements matter. The best philanthropic initiatives, time and again, are those where honest feedback occurs through meaningful measurements. For years, the world of philanthropy has believed that it is nearly impossible to measure social outcomes, but this belief is quickly changing. Financial investment funds, giving, and other tangible economic measures have been in place for years, but now new measurements (both quantitative and qualitative) are on the rise within mainstream philanthropy circles.

Quantitative Measurements

What is lacking cannot be counted.
—Ecclesiastes 1:15

Everything from dollars raised to dollars spent can be counted. But simply counting dollars raised or given is not enough. Jim Collins believes "performance must be assessed relative to mission, not financial returns" for nonprofits.[43] Collins' research shows "What matters is not finding the perfect indicator, but settling upon a *consistent and intelligent* method of assessing your output results, and then tracking your trajectory with rigor."[44] In other words, making a difference requires you to become personally involved with those you serve. Only when you are on the ground assessing and measuring, do you begin to see what works and what does not.

In Eric Thurman's article, *Performance Philanthropy: Bringing Accountability to Charitable Giving*, he reports the "Geneva Global has found that the highest return on investment is generated by local, grassroots organizations rather than big national agencies or international non-government organizations."[45] If the highest return on investment comes from local, grassroots organizations, then you must be with those you are serving.

Only when you are physically present with those you serve, does true accountability occur. This is why large national and international foundations tend to lose touch with both those they serve and those who give, because blind giving—writing checks without personal accountability eliminates the human touch of life. Why is this so important? When you get to know the people you serve, you get to know what they want, rather than assume that you *know* what they want. This is a basic entrepreneurial principle. And similarly, social entrepreneurs and philanthropic capitalists are bringing financial principles and capitalistic thinking to the world of philanthropy. With venture philanthropic thinking, measurements count.

These individuals measure their clientele, and they deliver what their clientele wants. Instead of viewing the recipients of charity as dependents, philanthropic leaders see them as independent, contributing members of society, with whom you can engage beyond handouts.

The old model of charity assumes that everyone wants the same meal, the same drink, the same Christmas gift, and the same clothes to wear. Charities then set a goal, raise the money, buy and/or have the supplies donated. Finally, the aid is distributed to needy dependent men, women, and children around the world. Afterwards, this type of philanthropic leader counts the amount of money and supplies collected. They met their goal, exceeded it, or sadly fell short. They measure how many stomachs they fed, bodies they clothed, and toys they distributed. By generating a nice report with photos they are able to attempt to raise the bar, and next year use the report as a marketing tool to drum up even more money and donated goods. This is the typical, traditional way of measuring outcomes from a numerical point of view. Finally, to beef up their marketing materials, they share a few heartfelt stories in hopes of raising more money. Cleary, this is an oversimplification of how many organizations quantify their data. There are more sophisticated groups that hire universities, accounting firms, and other research centers to quantify their research in a more scientific way.

As you and others look beyond the old conventional methodology of counting receipts and people who simply received charity, consider the new way venture philanthropists are challenging the status quo: free markets produce life change, which makes a difference even among the poorest. Venture philanthropists are empowering people with the ability to choose what they want and how they receive what they want and need. This creates a life shift for charitable recipients as they are moved from being a passive community who waits on aid to arrive, to becoming contributing, self-sustaining human beings who improve their own lives and communities. At this point, concerns of sustainability, long-term growth, and true value can begin to be quantified.

Since the old model assumes that every child wants the same Christmas gift, it is easy to calculate the number of toys donated and given to boys and girls around the world. But simply giving a toy at Christmas time, or calculating the number of turkeys given during the Thanksgiving Holiday, does not truly measure life change. Yes, it quantifies how many lives you touch in a day or holiday season, but it does not show if these people whom you served are truly better off from having received their turkey at Thanksgiving or their toy at Christmas.

IS THERE MORE?

The new role of quantitatively and qualitatively measuring outcomes will emerge once donors understand their customer. In society, "the for-profit world generally measures only economic value, while the nonprofit world (when it measures anything) generally only measures social value."[46] One of the new roles in which philanthropic leaders should engage in is to measure both the economic and social value. Research indicates "the most effective measure is the most *prima facie*: life change. This is, at heart, what philanthropy is all about—changing lives of the neediest among us."[47] Hence, everything from "income growth, improved nutrition, access to health care, orphans housed, AIDS patients cared for, access to clean water, completion of primary education, and falling infant mortality rates are clear indicators of life improvement that can be readily quantified."[48]

In order to quantify such results, philanthropic leaders should research charities and foundations in the same way as they would investigate for-profit companies. Ask lots of questions. How does the organization function? How much money goes to administrative overhead and how much goes to the actual work? What are the salaries of the executives? What is the track record for the charity? Current research indicates:

> Other key indicators are sustainability and scalability of the intervention, existence of thorough project plans with all-defined performance measures, and risk management planning. Project leaders themselves are strong indicators of future performance, all able to be measured through demonstrated experience, demonstrated commitment to power sharing and training of others, and extent of networking to other implementers. Nearly eighty percent of projects evaluated and funded over the past five years using this methodology met or exceeded their stated numerical project objectives.[49]

These types of measurements inform philanthropic leaders with feedback and accountability. Unfortunately, "lack of feedback is one of the most critical flaws in existing aid … because of the near-invisibility of efforts and results by aid agencies in distant parts of the world."[50] Nevertheless, when you get personally involved and actually know the people you serve, your personal involvement offsets any long-distant, remote form of feedback. Rather than having to wait on reports, you are there. You see with your own eyes and hear with your own ears. You know what works and what does not work, because your giving is deeply embedded within the action. Furthermore, you will want to understand the many connections of what is done versus what is actually achieved. By measuring inputs with results achieved, you will see how much it costs in manpower, dollars, and time to be able to reproduce results in the future.

The chronic mindset of "giving blindly" also encourages a "theory of hope," which simply hopes for the best without any real examination into systemic problems that a "theory of change" provides. To illustrate, what is the outcome between building a clean-water well if locals do not have water jugs or if the people cannot safely access such water because rebel forces are shooting them? Hence, a theory of change seeks to clearly look at all of the dynamics that underline poverty without espousing wishful thinking that money solves all global philanthropic initiatives.

In addition to these quantitative measures, philanthropic leaders should measure "cost per impact as the fundamental measure of any philanthropic investment," reports the Center for High Impact Philanthropy.[51] Even though this may appear to be in opposition to Jim Collins' research within social sectors, both schools of thought should be wrestled with. Rather than taking an either/or approach, your leadership will typically consist of paradoxical thinking as you test what fits best within your realm of influence. With that said, the Center for High Impact Philanthropy claims that cost per impact consists of two components: "1) social impact, as measured by specific, objective criteria for success; and 2) cost, as measured by the investments made by philanthropists or other sources to realize the impact."[52] When thinking about social impact, you need to ask questions about impact measures, such as cost per initiative in terms of dollars invested, time spent, and manpower needed. These questions inevitably lead you to ask quantitative questions concerning the cost per impact. Here, you should not only be concerned with maximizing money through strategic funding, but you should also be looking at the global economy, exchange rate on money, and the stability of geo-political demographics around the world. Because in a global society your philanthropic impact may reach beyond your local community to around the world, it is best to discern how the global economy impacts your work as well. By measuring the worth of the dollar against other currencies, especially if you are investing in global philanthropic initiatives, then you may find different seasons and times to be more beneficial to maximize funding.

Thus, philanthropic leaders should ask the hard questions in regard to cost per impact. As an example, you must discern not only the best measurements to use, but also the best time to implement certain philanthropic projects. This type of thinking requires discernment, wise leadership, and possibly brainstorming about the many uncertainties and possibilities that the future holds. Nevertheless, quantitative research only takes you so far, and then you should turn to qualitative research.

QUALITATIVE MEASUREMENTS

How has the quality of one's life changed as a result of your philanthropic leadership? Why should anyone follow you as a philanthropic leader? What difference have you made in the life of others? Questions like these bring us to the important issues of the heart and soul. At this stage, it is not about how much money you have given or how many mouths you have fed, or how many people you have reached. What is important is how both you and these recipients are different, better, and transformed from within as a result of your relationship of love. The quality of your leadership, the quality of your relationships, and the quality of your work as a philanthropist must be measured.

EXAMPLES OF QUALITATIVE MEASUREMENTS

The qualitative measures on social impact powerfully reveal the stories of changed lives. Often organizations document a specific individual's story through video to share with donors. Other organizations encourage donors to visit on-site with those they have helped. When this takes place, commitment strengthens, strategic involvement increases, and often transformation occurs in the donor's life. I met a young girl in Kenya who was brutally raped at the age of nine; she will forever walk with a limp. This young, crippled orphan continues to drive my personal philanthropic work, and she gives me the assurance that the organization I participate with is providing real help to the poor and oppressed. Personal experiences like this one often produces innovative thinking on behalf of the philanthropic leader. For example, rather than simply writing a check, one might realize you should offer your time, professional expertise, network, and awareness to maximize one's investment. The qualitative stories of changed lives often inspire a shared vision, encourage the heart, and challenge the philanthropic process while spurring philanthropic leaders to model the way for other leaders as they enable others to act.

The Quality of Your Leadership

Few people look forward to receiving their annual employment reviews outlining their work performance. But as the old saying goes, "what gets measured gets done" is true even when spoken about measuring the qualitative side of your leadership. The quality of your leadership ultimately begins with the character of your heart. Measuring your character may seem odd and rather obtrusive, but if you want to make a difference, if you choose to grow and develop into a mature, philanthropic leader, then I would suggest that the heart of your character is the most important place to start. It has been said, "The heart is deceitful above all things."[9] Because the heart can lead you to dishonest practices, it is easy to get caught up in the moment and begin to fall back into giving out of pride and selfishness. Or your temptation may be to give in order to mislead others with what appears to be a charitable spirit. Whatever the temptation, your heart can deceive you or others, so it is important that the quality of it remains in check. The acrostic *HEART* sums up the character needed for philanthropic leadership: *Humility, Empathy, Authenticity, Responsibility,* and *Trust*. The mature leader takes the initiative to measure these qualities first in their own leadership.

Humility, the Quality of Your Heart

Just as leadership begins with values, the quality of humility is the foundation of a solid heart bent on serving others in love. For the Christian philanthropic leader, humility ultimately drives the leader to continue his or her calling from a spirit of Christ. In other words, the quality of your leadership is focused on serving others rather than serving your own agenda. In addition, humility entails honesty because if you are guided by protecting your image as a leader, you may be tempted to be dishonest. Humility requires honesty. If you commit to living a life of humility, then you have nothing to hide. Yes, the truth hurts at times and it is difficult to clarify troubling concerns, but in the end, honesty is the best policy.

If the quality of your heart is not humble, then your ability to lead with honesty will be difficult. Others will notice, and your integrity as a leader

---

9 Jeremiah 17:9a, *New International Version.*

will suffer. So how can you effectively measure the quality of your honesty? The best way is by allowing your actions to mirror your words. By doing what you say, giving even when it hurts, and by fulfilling your promises is the beginning. Deep within your heart you know if you practice what you espouse or if you primarily pay lip service, and over time, others will know as well. If you have pledged to give a certain amount of money, time, or energy for a particular project, then you must fulfill your commitments. No one will follow your leadership if you continue to make excuse after excuse.

Living with humility entails more than simply living in alignment with your words and actions. In the words of Jesus, you must take a critical look at your own blind spots before trying to show others' theirs. Or to state it differently:

> By humility, we don't necessarily mean self-effacing modesty, but rather an ability not to be thrown off by the distortions of a big ego. You have to be able to take a dispassionate view of your strengths that takes into account your own limitations, whether they are imposed by your circumstances or a deeper part of your makeup.[53]

EMPATHY, THE QUALITY OF RELATING

Empathy is another character trait that you should model as a philanthropic leader. Empathy is the "ability to be aware of, to understand and to appreciate the feelings and thoughts of others," writes Stein and Book.[54] Leaders who reveal empathy hear the unvoiced questions, while anticipating the unvoiced needs. By discerning what is below the surface you are able to connect and relate on a deeper empathic level. Remember, philanthropy is about loving humankind; therefore, your leadership should manifest empathy for those with whom you serve alongside.

AUTHENTICITY MAKES A DIFFERENCE

But what character traits must the philanthropic leader manifest in order to love another deeply enough where human flourishing occurs?

First, the philanthropic leader acts with authenticity. Authenticity consists of alignment between one's words and actions. Second, as you lead your foundation or when you are on the mission field working among those you serve, your leadership should remain consistent. Who you are in a board meeting should reflect who you are in a soup kitchen feeding the hungry. You lead with an authentic quality that remains the same no matter what the situation. The quality and character of your leadership is consistent. This means you lead from being yourself, rather than trying to be someone else. Because philanthropic leadership is relational, you must be yourself. Your followers will know if you are trying to be someone else. And if they wanted to follow someone else, then they could. To illustrate, leaders who relate to their people's values authentically lead with credibility:

> Their everyday actions fit not only with their personal values but also with the values of the groups of which they are a part. Through continual observation and reflection, they know their priorities, their strengths and weaknesses. They increase commitment to common goals by genuinely talking and listening to the people they care most about. And they hold themselves and others accountable for pursuing valued goals.[55]

In other words, as leadership guru Warren Bennis once cited, "Authenticity ... cannot be faked. To be redundant, it's real."[56] So I ask you, is your leadership authentic? Do those around you believe you are real? Now is the time to measure your own performance as either an authentic or inauthentic philanthropic leader.

RESPONSIBILITY MAKES A DIFFERENCE

Responsibility is another character trait of philanthropic leadership. In a nutshell, if you desire to be a philanthropic leader, then you must practice responsibility. For leadership is being responsible for the decisions you make for others. With that said, the centrality of responsibility is accountability. You are accountable for not only how you lead, but also how you give as a leader. You are accountable for seeing that philanthropic projects are executed in a timely and appropriate manner. And if you are simply donating money to a public charity to carry out its mission, then it is your responsibility to hold that organization accountable for its actions. This means you do not tolerate excuses. Your responsibility and accountability should not tolerate excuses, but rather seek solutions as to why the leadership failed, a goal was not achieved, or a project was not completed. For too long, public nonprofit organizations have been allowed to slide because they do charitable work. But simply doing charitable work is no excuse for not doing it well.

Since leadership is situational and every situation is somewhat different, it is often the case that the leader will lack sufficient data when making a decision. As a result, the consequences of the decision may entail unforeseen negative results. But here again, it is your job as a philanthropic leader to oversee and be responsible when unforeseen negative results occur. Clearly, you will not always make the best decision, and you will not always lead with perfect performance, but you have no excuse in not owning up to your own failures. By admitting wrong, you are in a better position to take responsibility in the future.

TRUST MAKES A DIFFERENCE

Finally, the last character trait in the acrostic *HEART* is trust. Trust "is fragile. Like a piece of china, once cracked it is never quite the same. And people's trust in business, and those who lead it, is today cracking."[57] At the point of dishonesty, trust breaks. Telling the truth, as easy as it sounds, is often the hardest and most uncomfortable task of a leader. Nevertheless, you must take responsibility to lead an environment of trust with those you serve. This begins with you telling the truth by defining reality. It is not about how you wish things were but how things actually are. Because, more often than not, nonprofit leaders create an appearance that all is well, even when they are drowning in poor management, debt and unnecessary expenditures. It is your responsibility to seek the truth both in your foundation and those with whom you partner. This means holding both yourself and those among you accountable. By creating a context where truth and trust reign, you will have created a loving leadership environment. For where there is love, your people will not worry about hiding the truth. So my question is, how well do you lead with truth?

By examining the quality of your own leadership, you should have a good measurement on the character of your heart.

THE QUALITY OF YOUR RELATIONSHIPS

The quality of your relationships also needs measuring in order to best relate with your people, purpose, and overall progress within your foundation, charity, or cause. When you understand the importance of a purposeful relationship, then you should structure your people in order to execute a purpose where performance is measured over a period of time. Without people, an organization does not exist. Without purpose, an organization is stagnant. And if an organization is not structured to measure progress, then it may remain inept for adapting to performance goals. These three primary building blocks—people, purpose, and progress—act as the DNA elements of leadership. When you begin to view people, purpose, and progress through this triadic lens, then your leadership brings a holistic maturity to your work. And in maturity, you will realize that too often "organizations desire leaders but structure themselves in ways that kill leadership."[58] In order to prevent this fatality, you must understand the importance of structuring your people in such a way that progress occurs and your purposes are fulfilled. It is in this high exaltation of people, the dignity of humanity, where the relationship of leadership begins.

PEOPLE: YOUR INTERNAL EMPLOYEES MAKE A DIFFERENCE

Every foundation, charity, and philanthropic organization entails people. As a philanthropic leader, it is important to realize your own personal strengths, weaknesses, desires, and temptations. You must understand that you too share with everyone else this living dynamic called humanity. And the harmony of humanity can create a symphony when followers respect their leaders because they understand how much their leaders truly care for them. True leaders do not simply make photo op appearances; they rub shoulders with those whom they work.

Because leadership is a relational participatory engagement between the leader and the led, your perception of this dynamic is critical to the position (placement of power), profession (placement of expertise) and panel (placement of team players) of your overall organizational structure. The placement of power reveals the hierarchical position of each employee. In a traditional foundational design, the executive director holds the top position. This communicates to everyone in the foundation the hierarchy of responsibility in conjunction with their particular position. However, philanthropic leaders may also position their people according to their particular expertise. For example, if one's profession is accounting, then the accountant often becomes the chief financial officer. Since people bring different skill sets to an organization, the philanthropic leader is responsible for strategically placing each person within the organization according to their skills. In his book, *Good to Great*, Jim Collins uses a bus as an example of an organizational structure. Here you may have the wrong people on the bus, the right people on the bus but in the wrong place, or you may have both the wrong people in the wrong seats. Collins' point is that when companies get the right people on the bus in the right positions, and the wrong people off, then the organization gains momentum. This occurs because even if the structure (i.e., the bus) is broken, you already have the right people who desire to fix it or completely change structures. Furthermore, the organization gains momentum because as Collins espouses, "the right people don't need to be tightly managed or fired up; they will be self-motivated by the inner drive to produce the best results and to be part of creating something great."[59] I have witnessed this time and again within healthy nonprofits. People simply perform and serve out of love for the work, which is a direct relation to their skills, talents, and giftedness.

Lastly, internal employees often work in groups on a panel, board, or special task force where they collaborate together as team players. For example, development relation teams often work in collaboration to raise funds. Although this triadic pairing of position (control), profession (autonomy), and panel (cooperation) illustrates the internal people (i.e., employees) to your organization, a philanthropic leader should also consider external people (i.e., those external to your direct leadership).

PEOPLE: YOUR EXTERNAL CUSTOMER
MAKES A DIFFERENCE

External people consist of anyone outside the organization. This includes the community, customers and/or recipients of philanthropy, and collaborative alliances. The community is a powerful external force of people who can either add or subtract value to your philanthropic organization. If the community perceives something they do not like about a charity, then the community may protest, cease volunteering, and stop financially supporting it. The customers of a philanthropic organization or charity consist of the people who directly receive the benefits (i.e., products and services) from the organization. Hence, it is important to remember that the customer shapes the organizational structure of your foundation. Here again, it is the work of people and not the amount of money you have that determines your effectiveness as a philanthropic leader. Finally, collaborative partners act as third party suppliers, corporate sponsors, or even strategic alliances bringing a wealth of knowledge, network, and skills.

STRUCTURING MAKES A DIFFERENCE

If you are going to engage others via participatory action, then you need to choose a strategy and structure that allows for freedom, flexibility, and faith. Loving and leading others in such a way whereby you do not impose your agenda, but rather allow for the participants to engage the process may appear chaotic, unstructured, or ever-changing like a chameleon. However, participatory action allows everyone to engage the process from their strengths, so that the overall group goals are reached. The structure you create should complement rather than hinder the process. Outcome measurements may indicate that you need to adapt your structure along the way. If the current structure is not producing the desired results, then it might be time to listen to those under your leadership to learn how they would structure the charity or foundation to maintain maximum efficiency and effectiveness.

PEOPLE: YOUR RELATING POINT MAKES A DIFFERENCE

All great leaders understand that people matter. You should consider the people you serve as the primary jewel of your philanthropy. If people are your most valuable asset because they are the contact with customers, the relating point, then clearly your organizational structure must factor in the relational dynamics of people. What is a relating point? A relating point is the point where the phenomenon of relating occurs. This encompasses the many dynamics of relationality. Relational dynamics consist of the fact that people relate to themselves, other people, and they may also relate to a higher power. When people relate to themselves, Aristotle claims people relate in three ways: they relate to reason (logos), emotions (pathos), and behavior (ethos).[60] To illustrate, some donors only want to know the numbers and hard data when researching a charity to invest in. These individuals want logical and intellectual reasons for getting involved. However, some people are emotionally enraptured to work with a particular cause or charity when they see, feel, and experience the need. Just as the root word for "pathos" sounds, it is used to describe pathology or suffering. When people feel the suffering of children in an orphanage or women dying of breast cancer in a hospital wing, these individuals will be passionately moved to give. Finally, the ethos or ethic of an organization may cause some philanthropic leaders to get connected because they see the need as being an ethical or moral obligation to meet. For example, many nonprofit health clinics in America exist because people hold a moral obligation to promote free health care for the poor. In addition, from mentoring to modeling right behavior to those around you as a philanthropic leader, your own personal ethics are always at stake.

This three-dimensional perspective also reveals how people think from a mental intelligence, emotional intelligence, and moral intelligence. You may find it beneficial to measure the performance and wellness of each type of intelligence to best connect your people to their strengths. From personality tests to emotional intelligence and moral intelligence testing, both you and those you serve may benefit from these types of instruments.

PEOPLE: COOPERATION MAKES A DIFFERENCE

There are two types of cooperation. One type is relational cooperation where people interact with each other to perform a particular task; the other type of cooperation is purposeful. Purposeful cooperation takes place when two or more employees work for the same mission of the charity, while these employees may never actually engage each other face to face. In large global philanthropic organizations where thousands of people are employed, the executive leadership team may never know the custodial engineering team, but both teams work for the betterment of the organization.

PROGRESS: A LEARNING ORGANIZATION MAKES A DIFFERENCE

Every organization should be a learning organization, where the leader tracks organizational progress and performance. Progress is the control aspect of your design. The design entails processes for managing information, maximizing technology, and maturing leaders. Intangible resources like time, space, information, emotions and spirituality also impact a learning organization. For example, managing information gives control over what should be known and to whom, and how information is going to be controlled. In a virtual design foundation, where people primarily interact through technology, an organization's information may entail a computer server where everyone can log in, or just specific people may access. To continue with the technology example of a virtual organization, all organizational structures should maximize the advances in technology as best suited for them. Is your structure designed for learning, progress, and measurability to occur at all levels? Hence, you may measure the degree by which your charity or foundation grows through learning.

LEADERSHIP EXERCISE

Robert Greenleaf asked the following pivotal question:

> Do those served grow as persons; do they, while being
> served, become healthier, wiser, freer, more autonomous,
> more likely themselves to become servants? And, what is
> the effect on the least privileged in society; will he benefit,
> or, at least, will he not be further deprived?[61]

For today's exercise, ponder this question as it relates to how you
measure your philanthropic activities. Will the money and leadership
given, help the people you serve grow, become healthier, wiser, freer, more
autonomous, more likely themselves to become donors too? Will funding
this project actually benefit the least privileged in society, or will it entrap
them to a life of destitution? What do you need to implement in order to
take the necessary responsibility to ensure transformational results from
your leadership? What quantitative and qualitative measurements do you
need to implement today?

Feedback, Accountability, & Responsibility

Rank does not confer privilege or give power. It imposes responsibility.
—Peter Drucker

Exercising responsibility is essential to healthy philanthropic leadership. It is your responsibility to seek out feedback and hold charities, foundations, and board members accountable for their actions. Wasting resources often creates a culture where more waste is produced without accountability or thought. Mass mail going to one's donor base, and money spent on donors in the hopes of raising more money, continues to be two major drivers of wastefulness within nonprofit organizations. As charities strive to grow bigger and bigger they tend to do so by adding fat rather than lean muscle. Rather than becoming stronger, healthier, and fitter organizations with growth, these groups tend to lose the importance of responsible feedback and accountability. In 2009, a public charity decided to reduce costs by ceasing to mail a monthly newsletter and support envelope to its donor base. After eight months into the year, this organization did not experience any decline in their monthly financial support. Now it exclusively uses the Internet to connect with their donor base while saving thousands of dollars by eliminating direct mail.

Actively pursuing feedback and holding nonprofits accountable is the ethical sphere of philanthropic leadership. If you do not take the initiative to scrutinize the results of nonprofit promises, then, by default, you are in contempt of endorsing a culture where the doors are open for everything from passivity to board criminality. Board members, executive directors, and development directors must be held accountable for all of the work they espouse. This is not only your ethical calling as a donor, but also as a board member, friend, or partner to any nonprofit organization.

When Bernie Madoff was caught in the largest Ponzi scheme of $50 billion, many charities, private foundations, and other philanthropic initiatives were ruined by his ruthless deception and theft. You must scrutinize money managers and other stockbrokers who may not directly work for your foundation, but who, like Madoff, can radically impact your philanthropic work. Madoff's irresponsible, illegal, and immoral behavior caused many nonprofit organizations harm, and it is a reminder to you that even fraudulent behavior occurring outside your organization can impact your foundation or charity, which will require diligent leadership from you. As a result, your character as a philanthropic leader depends on your ability to seek honest feedback and to take the necessary steps in being a responsible steward.

Being dishonest once, often leads down a slippery slope to more dishonesty. With enough time, you will hear something to the tune of "the problem we are facing is not simply black and white, right or wrong. You know, there are lots of grey areas." Or, "we tried to reach our goals, but we simply did not receive enough funding." Or, "I don't recall you earmarking that check to go specifically to that particular project. If we messed up, sorry, we'll make sure it does not happen again."

When leaders in the nonprofit world lack brutal honesty, they not only hurt themselves, their organization, and the broader charitable community, they also hurt those they serve. In addition, when you encounter nonprofit leaders who cannot be honest with you, when they skirt issues, act as if your questions and concerns do not matter, or evade honest dialogue and inquiry, then your leadership will be challenged.

Because honesty is one of the most pressing issues today, it is vital that your words align with your values, beliefs, and actions. By developing your ability to frame your actions and words within a context that creates an honest depiction of reality, you will clear the way for open, honest, and safe dialogue. This requires you to balance both your perspective and those you disagree with in a way that reflects reality. In other words, are you able to clearly see both sides of the story without attacking the person? As Stephen Covey puts it, "Honesty is telling the truth—in other words, *conforming our words to reality.* Integrity is *confronting reality to our words*—in other words, keeping promises, and fulfilling expectations."[62] When this type of contextual clarity occurs, then you and your organization will begin to experience honest dialogue.

Once again, this is easier said than done. The more money at stake and the bigger the misguided assumptions, the harder it is to emotionally see current reality in a way that brings integrity to a problem. As you are on your philanthropic leadership journey, do not be surprised when current reality does not live up to all the grand goals of your nonprofit. For example, I recently received a letter saying how a particular organization would train over 100,000 people in India, while also caring for over 300,000 children. These numbers are grand and glorious and may be good at generating donations, but in all likelihood, this particular organization does not have the infrastructure, systems, or manpower to execute such lofty goals. In other words, their grant letter is not honest and does not align with current reality. In addition, letters like these rarely have third party audits that provide honest feedback from both quantitative and qualitative outcomes. In order to prevent this, it is your responsibility to ask such questions way before handing over money, time, and/or energy to such endeavors.

REFLECTION AND ADAPTATION

And time for reflection with colleagues is for me a lifesaver; it is not just a nice thing to do if you have the time. It is the only way you can survive.
—Margaret J. Wheatley

Philanthropic leadership does not end with the completion of a project, volunteering your time to a certain initiative, or giving money to reach a certain fundraising goal. Philanthropic leadership truly begins when you reflect on the results of each project, initiative, or goal. When you take the time to analyze both successes and failures and how you could make proper adjustments, then you are on the way to becoming a mature philanthropic leader. Knowing where, when, why, and how to adapt for future improvement starts as you take the time to reflect. You must also take the time to reflect on the relationships of the lives you have touched and those who have touched you. Reflecting on how you have changed in relation with others is the beginning of a more holistic understanding of what it means to be a philanthropic leader.

The intentional practice of reflection should become a continuous process of your thinking, leading, and living. As you make sense of your experiences and relationships as a leader, you will learn how to better connect, relate, and love those you serve. For it is in reflection that you begin to see things more clearly, completely, and concisely. Having a clear, concise, and complete picture in your mind creates a type of movie picture, where each frame, when played in your mind, gives you a story to share with others. Sharing your stories of principles learned, people loved, and progress achieved should bring others into the fold of philanthropy. For me, the opportunity to reflect and think deeply about previous experiences becomes a powerful tool when my reflections are shared to spur others on. Either to warn friends from making common mistakes or to encourage them to make a difference, sharing your reflective insights and being able to adapt accordingly will sharpen your skills and acumen as a leader.

> ## LIFE PRINCIPLE: FOR IT IS IN REFLECTION THAT YOU BEGIN TO SEE THINGS MORE CLEARLY, COMPLETELY, AND CONCISELY

Revisiting your actions as they apply to your core values and beliefs is a critical point to enhancing your future leadership as a philanthropist. Did you engage in some activity that you were not completely sold on? How did you get yourself in such a place and how did it make you feel? How could you have responded differently in order to participate in alignment with your values and beliefs? Questions like these help clarify issues you may have already experienced or will experience in the future. As you revisit different encounters you have had with difficult people or compromising circumstances, attempt to look at your own weaknesses and strengths. You may find that it is easier to say no to funding requests if you have a board that can filter your requests. You may find that someone on your team is better at communicating the values of your foundation in a way that does not compromise the integrity of your mission and vision. Look at every opportunity as a learning experience to reflect on. You may not see everything while you are in the heat of the moment, but once you allow the dust to settle and you begin to reflect, you will see things in a new light.

Rereading granting and funding requests is another way you can reflect on what others are truly asking from you. I find that most people truly do not read the piles of funding requests they receive, but when they do, they often see poor logical arguments explaining why organizations need certain amounts of your money to function in certain ways. Philanthropic leaders who are skilled business people tend to have an eye for reading between the lines of the requests they receive. And the more you read them, and the more you reflect upon them, the better you will understand that the majority of all public charities tend to view money as the only tool for survival, success, and sustainability. When you do the math, follow up by asking the hard questions. You may discover that little thought has been given to the long-term use of your donation. Yet, if these organizations have thought of creative ways to operate, ensuring that one day they will not need your money, then you may find yourself willing to help them now to reach future self-sustainability.

LEADERSHIP EXERCISE

Take an hour today to do nothing but reflect on your philanthropic leadership. Intentionally look at your strengths, weaknesses, opportunities, and threats. In other words, implement an old fashioned SWOT (Strengths, Weaknesses, Opportunities, Threats) analysis of what is working and why? Look for areas that need to be adapted. Ask yourself tough questions and look for answers from both sides—see the answers in a new light. Today's hour is only the beginning. It is crucial for philanthropic leaders to continually reflect and adapt. Make an appointment on a certain day of the week or month to reflect on your purpose, people, and progress within your sphere of influence. Make this a special time where interruptions do not occur. If necessary, go to some remote place where you can journal your thoughts.

Chapter Five:
The Future of Philanthropy

We thought we had the answers, it was the questions we had wrong.
—Bono

T HE FUTURE OF PHILANTHROPY RESTS in the questions we ask today. If we ask one set of questions, then we will lean toward a particular future. If we ask a different set of questions, then likewise, we will lean toward a different future. This is why it is so important to understand how your values shape and inform your thinking. For the questions you ignore, invite, or defer to, impact the answers to life's biggest challenges.

Insightful philanthropic leaders use scenario planning to create a diversity of possible futures. Within the field of philanthropy, three of the following scenarios illustrate different current pictures of philanthropy. The *conventional future* is the historical and traditional future of philanthropy. The *counter future* attempts to replace it while improving upon the conventional future. And then finally, the *creative future* brings radical innovation to social change via new questions.

The Future of Philanthropy

Real generosity toward the future lies in giving all to the present.
—Albert Camus

The future of philanthropy begins with you. Now more than ever, as the world faces a global economic meltdown, foresight, discernment, and the ability to see trends, patterns, and possible outcomes is paramount to preparing for the future. Without understanding the current times, you will find it difficult to properly navigate into the future. As you go down the road, what you see, as well as what you do not see, is critical to how you lead your organization and life forward. This is more than having a twenty-year strategic plan, this is more than establishing a large endowment fund with strategic purposes, and this is more than having your estate planning in order. The future of philanthropy depends on your foresight, your ability to see the unseen and adapt accordingly.

Foresight reflects on past movements, seeks present trends and current indicators, while casting multiple scenarios and plausible visions of what the future could bring. Your ability to examine driving forces both internal and external to your control, gives you the ability to understand how what happens on Wall Street could very likely impact your charitable endeavors on Main Street. When you intentionally maintain a pulse on global events, wild cards like international terrorism and socio-political changes, your philanthropic leadership strategies will give you a competitive edge in our ever-changing world. Just as many public nonprofits lost pledged monies in the weeks and months following 9/11, so too President Barrack Obama's administration may alter your philanthropic strategies. In other words, the world and all that is in it, continues to change and impact different sectors, which at first glance you may not think has any bearing on you. However, we ultimately live in a world of multiple layers of connectivity. And it is in maneuvering through all of these connections that hindsight, insight, and foresight are needed to bring the future of philanthropy into a place of strength rather than weakness.

Having the strength to sustain economic downturns, more terrorism, and other forms of economic fraud, is not so much contingent upon how much money you have, how endowed your foundation is, or how successful you were in the past at generating income, but rather, your ability to maintain long-term sustainability and transformation for the good of others depends on your ability to lead now. As long as life seems to be a happy and nice place where all is well, your leadership is not truly tested. But the test of your leadership is not how well you survive through the struggles and turmoil of life, but how well you prepared and planned when life is good. And this requires the discipline of practicing foresight.

You probably have already been practicing foresight throughout your life, without even realizing it. When you read the newspaper, watch the news, engage others in conversation, observe new construction going up in your community, and reflect on what is occurring in society and the world at large, you have actually exercised thoughtful foresight. You may have found yourself scratching your head at some situation that simply does not make sense. You may have even created multiple scenarios as you say, "what if we did x, or what if we gave x amount of money, or what if we could reduce poverty by seventy-five percent in the next ten years." Statements like these get your mind thinking about possible future events that you can control to some degree. Exercises like these, thinking about how today's current events impact tomorrow, and how today's actions carry future consequences, all point to the practice of futuring.

Futuring is not predicting what will happen tomorrow, nor is futuring the ability to look into a crystal ball to see the future. Futuring is not espousing religious prophetic revelations either. And futuring is not about executing your twenty-year plan to perfection. Futuring is the ability to perceive what could be in the future depending on the decisions you make today. Futuring does not ignore the present or forget the past, but rather the act of practicing foresight enables you to hold both perspectives in balance as you look ahead. You may find it helpful to challenge past and present assumptions about life, money, the poor, giving, and every other sphere of life that you find prudent to the future. When you find yourself asking strategic questions, while refusing to settle for pedestrian answers, then you are on your way to leading others into the future of greater human potentiality. Or you may simply find the past has a place of comfort to replicate in the future. This may serve you well for a while, but it often comes with a greater price—namely, your blindness to the long view. Or you may find your spirit reacting against the ways of the past and present in the hopes of living life and practicing philanthropy differently. You may be tired of hearing the Salvation Army bells ringing during the holidays to the point where you resist this type of charitable fundraising.

Whatever the case may be, three futures ultimately exist: 1) the conventional future, 2) the counter future, and 3) the creative future. The conventional future simply resembles the past and often looks like the present. The counter future resists practicing philanthropy the same way your grandparents did. And the creative future is full of innovation and ideas. It does not simply counter the conventional ways of thinking, but rather the creative future creates new systems of thought and action for improving the lives of others.

THE CONVENTIONAL FUTURE

I've seen the future and it's much like the present only longer.
—Dan Quisenberry

The conventional future of philanthropy is solely focused on money. This is nothing more than "philanthropy" being synonymous with giving money away, raising money, and needing money to do good work. In other words, the centrality of philanthropy is all about money. Your progress as a donor is measured by how much money you have given within a year, and how much your giving increased to a particular organization from last year. This becomes the primary standard for measuring success. If your foundation only gives the minimum five percent required by law, then you are operating in the conventional future.

In many ways the conventional future looks like the Vanderbilt family, Rockefellers and Carnegies of old. They used much of their fortunes to construct lasting buildings for public and private use, which forever beholds their names. From beautiful music performances held in Carnegie Hall to the regular *NBC Nightly News* broadcast from the infamous Rockefeller Center to the University of Vanderbilt standing proudly in Nashville, no one can argue that this traditional use of philanthropy continues to serve the greater good. This type of outcome has a place in philanthropy.

Other conventional and traditional means of philanthropy do come seasonal with the ringing bells from the Salvation Army to the selling of those delicious Girl Scout Cookies. A neighbor of mine even buys their Christmas tree every year from the Boy Scouts. From local PTA cookie drive fundraisers to the lavish over-the-top black-tie galas, what all of these traditional means of raising money have in common is that they are vividly red, white, and blue. This type of philanthropy is American and goes toward good American causes. Because of the very nature of needing to always raise more money, this conventional future establishes traditions, which continue on into the future. Every year, I know there are some fundraisers that I must attend, because it makes people feel good to see me there supporting their causes. It is like a traditional family reunion, but now the family is composed of your local donors, philanthropists, and civic-minded socialites.

The all not-so-powerful and mightily deceptive pledge card and matching donor dollar schemes also fall under the traditional mechanisms of getting your money. These programs usually come with fundraising gurus and expert consultants who also receive a percentage of your donation. These fundraising campaigns generate lots of excitement around everything from corporate picnics to grand entertainment. With emotions running high about future worship centers for churches, community parks, or hospital extension wings, you have the opportunity to invest in the future of someone's dream, new building, or program. And it makes so much sense on the surface to simply turn in your pledge card, because like shopping, no money is needed for the first down payment. All that is needed now is your pledge to give. Once the air has left the balloons, and the glitter from the fireworks is gone, then they come calling and sending you letter after letter to remind you of your pledge. The only problem is now the economy does not look so good, you are having second thoughts about what you pledged, and your heart has moved on. But the guilt to give remains and so you reluctantly believe that your gift must be given, your word must be kept, and hopefully all will be well.

But is all truly well? Didn't we give last year to the children? And why does it always appear to be the children who are in need? And who are these children anyway? Where are their parents? You think, "I can barely afford to give my own kids what they want, much less all of these other children, and even my children have heard me say no." These are many of the thoughts and questions you experience in the traditional world of philanthropy, and before you know it, another natural disaster strikes and you are called on to help save the world.

When disasters strike from Haiti's catastrophic earthquake to Hurricane Katrina in the Gulf of Mexico to horrific tsunamis on the shores of Indonesia, the conventional philanthropic leaders respond in the same old conventional ways. The celebrity telethon gets on the national and local television networks drumming up dollars for relief. Movie stars from Ben Affleck to Bruce Willis have taken your calls at such events, while famous musicians from Paul Simon to Rod Stewart sing in the hopes that you will ring up and give your credit card donation. Even though this type of fundraising format is relatively new in regard to cable television, you may have witnessed this now conventional method on several occasions. These pleas for your contribution often do well as they maximize the use of images to capture your emotions. When you see starving children in Africa with swollen stomachs and when you see the devastation from the aftermath of hurricanes, the images combined with the music and a powerful celebrity generates instant giving.

As the stars come out, this type of philanthropy is like a shot in the arm. It generates a lot of hype and money, but for the most part, very few donors ever participate beyond giving their credit card. In the case with the Katrina Fund, large, well known, and heavily endowed charities like the Red Cross and Salvation Army are the first tiered beneficiaries. And when America participates in giving to one or two organizations on such a large national scale, the proper measurements for accountability and feedback simply get deferred to those organizations that received the funds. The problem with this is, if you care about feedback, accountability, and measurable results and outcomes, you will have an extremely difficult time finding any satisfactory answers. However, if the goal is only to generate as much money in the shortest amount of time, then you will most likely consider yourself a success. The only problem is that this conventional methodology continues to demand more out of your wallet as the next wildfire strikes, hurricane hits, or tornado whips through your community.

Because storms continue to strike and natural disasters occur, it is critical to understand these wild cards of life sometimes come in fairly predictable ways. For those living in Florida, they know that the official hurricane season lasts from the first of June to the end of November. With this type of trend, foresight provides you with the ability to lead through turbulent times rather than simply reacting in chaotic and confused ways. The same is true for the philanthropic leader who lives in the conventional world of thought. You already know that the majority of public charities need to finish strong at the end of the year, so you should not be surprised as the year-end giving requests arrive in the mail. Likewise, if your philanthropic leadership entails feeding the homeless or providing a warm cup of hot coffee to the needy in winter, then you prepare your giving and serving accordingly to the seasonal calendar. You should not be rounding up more heavy blankets to give out this year simply because you did not think it would snow, or realize too late that you do not have safe havens for the homeless during a tornado or hurricane. Although these points seem obvious and even ridiculous to state, many charitable organizations continue to find themselves in a bind year after year, when the seasons of the life cycle occur.

Why does this happen? Many nonprofit organizations simply ride into the future on the coattails of their wealthy board members, while others pray for miraculous money to simply appear from a genie. Either complaining that it so hard to get volunteers to help, or donors to give more and larger amounts of money, the same old conversations, beliefs, and assumptions continue to reappear year after year. And then finally, philanthropic leaders, board members, and donors simply say enough is enough. But only when people get tired enough of staying stuck in the same old rut, do you see a new possible future emerge.

LEADERSHIP EXERCISE

1. What strengths do you see in the conventional future?
2. What weaknesses do you see in the conventional future?
3. How can you apply the strengths of the conventional future to your thinking?
4. What must you do to prevent these weaknesses from the conventional future from occurring?
5. What local, national, and global trends do you currently believe may impact your foundation in the future?

THE COUNTER FUTURE

It is said that the present is pregnant with the future.
—Voltaire

The counter future is a direct reaction to the conventional future. The counter future is tired of the same old song and dance. Rather than the joys and pleasures of the seasonal giving opportunities, those events now seem like a guilty manipulative force from which you cannot escape. What once was delight has now become your duty. As you see the yearly charity holiday gala quickly approaching, you scramble to find a way to be out of town. It is not that you really want to take a winter vacation; you just do not want to keep the conventional future alive. You find yourself with donor fatigue and even when you call into the local soup kitchen to serve, they don't want you, because so many volunteers have already rolled out for the holidays. But they still want your money.

Another request in the mail and another request hits the trash can. You think, "If I ran my business and house like this charity runs its organization, I too would be broke, and no one is going to send me a nice bonus check in the mail. No one is going to underwrite my year end short fall." If these thoughts and feelings have found their way into the deep recesses of your soul, then you are on the verge of not losing your mind; you are giving birth to a new future of philanthropy.

As with any birth, the pains to bring new life, a new way, a new order of things is one of the most excruciating events you will go through as a philanthropic leader. The old habits, thoughts, beliefs, assumptions, and values begin to be challenged, changed, and given freedom to live and die on their own. This of course takes time, patience, and the strength to step back to see the bigger picture. This does not mean that your days of donating money are gone, but this does mean that you may temporarily take a vacation from your financial giving. As you step away, many individuals and organizations may pressure you to give, which you have supported in the past. Just let these groups know that you are taking a pause in funding right now. Some relationships may be forever severed, but I argue that those individuals probably were never your true friends. But your true friends will continue to be there for you even when you have stopped supporting their causes, charities, and organizations. And as you step back, you may find that your calling to be a philanthropic leader grows sharper, more intense, and more focused. It is here through the long birth pains of being the lonely sojourner that you begin to discover creative and innovative ways of being a philanthropic leader as a reaction to the traditions of old.

LIFE PRINCIPLE: BY SUPPORTING COMPANIES THAT SUPPORT SOCIAL CAUSES, YOU BECOME PHILANTHROPIC AS A CONSUMER

In the counter future of philanthropy, you may find yourself being a tad selfish when it comes to your giving. You want to give to help others, but you also want to be helped. Instead of writing that big check, you now make that big donation on your American Express card to receive all of those frequent flyer points. You give and you get. Or you and your family go on a trip with a cause. Rather than paying for someone else to go on a short-term mission trip, you decide to go yourself. Instead of taking the family to the Ritz-Carlton or the Four Seasons for another lavish vacation, you take the family on a mission to serve others in places like Africa or South America. You rough it for a week or two and receive an enormous blessing by working with the poor. You feel good that you have instilled values into your children and that you have contributed by the sweat of your brow. More than putting your hard labor into your acts of kindness, you want to share with others that you truly care.

In the conventional future, if you were to share with others that you care, then you would give so that your name, company's logo, and pride would shine in the spotlight of being one of the largest donors. You may select a certain level of giving to have your name inscribed on a park bench or you may give more money to see your name engraved in cement on the donor wall of fame. But in the counter future, you resent this type of giving. Nevertheless, you want to inspire others to participate and be concerned for the less fortunate. So, it is here, where new ideas in recent years have emerged like Product (RED), which sells clothes, sneakers, cell phones, and computers in the marketplace, and a portion of the sale proceeds goes to Africa to help people dying of HIV/AIDS. Or you intentionally decide to purchase your socially conscious bottled water from Starbucks. Ethos Water helps children around the world get clean water while raising awareness of the World Water Crisis.[63] So rather than sending money to help build a clean water well, you buy yourself a bottle of water to raise awareness. This type of counter reaction against conventional means of giving may give you a nice warm feeling inside and it may temporarily quench your thirst. Unfortunately, how do you feel when you, the consuming philanthropist, realize that Starbucks wastes approximately 6 million gallons of water each day?[64] Is this the type of reaction that a counter future brings? Starbucks stores run water continuously to prevent their taps from contamination. The amount of water wasted by Starbucks is enough to quench the thirst of Namibia's drought stricken people.[65] Stories like Starbucks wasting water as they attempt to find ways to promote clean water for the poor seem incompatible and inauthentic to their values. This is not to say that all initiatives from both the corporate world and the philanthropic world produce questionable behavior. It only reveals inconsistencies that may occur even in the counter future. For it is better to be proactionary than simply reactionary.

The labor and innovation of Bono has proven noble and creative with Product (RED). It is clear that the funds from selling (RED) goods and services pay pharmaceutical companies for anti-malaria and antiretroviral therapy among HIV/AIDS patients. Maybe one day these pharmaceutical companies will establish manufacturing facilities in places like Africa where the locals can participate in the production and education of these drugs. This way, the economy in the developing world can benefit and bring about social and economic change. Thinking like this usually occurs in the creative future of philanthropy.

LEADERSHIP EXERCISE

1. Describe how you have participated in the counter future. What did you do as a reaction to the conventional future?

2. What aspects do you particularly like about the counter future? How might you apply this to your leadership?

3. From your own philanthropic journey, what have you participated in as a reaction to something you experienced?

4. How can you ensure that your support of a good cause is truly authentic? Are you willing to do the necessary research about companies that promote philanthropy?

5. What policies and procedures do you need to establish in order to lead ethically and morally?

THE CREATIVE FUTURE

In each action we must look beyond the action at our past, present,
and future state, and at others whom it affects, and see the
relations of all those things. And then we shall be very cautious.
—Blaise Pascal

The creative future looks and acts very differently from the conventional and counter future. Even though creativity and innovation spring up within the conventional and counter future, these futures, though not necessarily bad or wrong in and of themselves, seem to fall short of empowering those it attempts to serve. The conventional future and the counter future of philanthropy serve themselves and the almighty dollar. The creative future of philanthropy stands in opposition to the established norms of giving; it looks beyond money to the heart of people. It is here, where Muhammad Yunus, one of the greatest heroes of philanthropy has risen high by kneeling low. Yunus understands that there are no quick fixes and no smiley-faced band-aids for some of the world's greatest people who happen to be caught in the cycle of poverty and oppression. He realizes that the journey is long and caution is required, because your leadership matters to others.

NEW PARADIGMS

Yunus, considered the banker to the poor, imagined a future that was radically different from anything else he had ever seen. As the banking world looked upon the poor as being unworthy of credit, Yunus believed they were worthy of credit. As many assumed that the poor have a lazy work ethic, Yunus believed the poor work harder than most. As the world treated the poor as being only good for receiving handouts, Yunus empowered the poor with dignity, believing they could not only make a difference in the world, but also that we can learn from them. As the paradigms of philanthropic thinking shift, former defeatist assumptions get replaced with hopeful ones, and a bright future begins to emerge. But this takes an honest look at the past and present to understand the limiting beliefs and values. Once these limiting beliefs and values are exchanged with new empowering beliefs and values, then the creative future begins to unfold.

Historically in Western civilization, it is the male who makes a living to provide for the economic needs of his family. Even as this traditional model slowly shifts in the West, in other parts of the world, particularly in Africa, the woman plays a vital role of responsible leadership in the household. Yunus' research and work in Bangladesh reveals that women are more likely to succeed in being responsible stewards over financial concerns than men.[66] As a result, by empowering women with jobs in which they control the cash, projects, and strategies of operations, they continue to prove that they are not only credit worthy, but also wise, intelligent, and responsible entrepreneurs. This may be due to the belief that many women are hardwired with a motherly tendency to care for others, even when it is a sacrifice to their own well-being. Or this may be due to the belief that a woman's tendency is not to squander any amount of extra surplus on what have traditionally been men's activities like gambling, drinking, and carousing. Whatever the factors at play, the qualitative research reveals again and again that women, especially among the extreme poor, tend to take a more fiduciary responsible role than men. Of course this is not to say that all men are one particular way or that all women are another. It is only to say that poor women from an overall perspective are making greater progress than men when it comes to the developing world.

Many women take charge of their homes, their entrepreneurial micro-businesses, and their community. Rose, a Burundian lady, came to our home with a friend to share her story. Rose lived through the 1994 Rwandan genocide, and today she has a small clothing business. With initial start-up help from our friend, Rose was able to start a sewing business making clothes and selling them. Now she hires other women in her village. By teaching them how to sew and make goods, they are able to make a profit. Rose's community no longer has to wait for donated clothes to travel from all parts of the world to perhaps reach them, they are now interdependent among each other and independent from charitable clothing donations. Stories like this help bring awareness, hope, and encouragement that the future of philanthropy is empowering, transforming, and bringing new sustainable living to the extreme poor.

SCENARIOS

Scenarios play a major role in the future of philanthropy. Scenarios are nothing more than stories of possible futures. Great stories give vivid details, twists and turns, while portraying a particular future. The use of scenarios in your leadership tool kit aids decision-making, spurs creative thinking, and continues to challenge your assumptions and beliefs about plausible outcomes. By creating stimulating and strategic scenarios, your philanthropic future should not amaze you when it arrives.

Even though scenarios are only stories about what could be, it is important to realize that the stories you tell and how you tell them inform your actions today. From shaping policy and procedure guidelines to setting goals to daydreaming about what you would do if you had more money, more time, more people, and more knowledge shapes your thinking and how you see the world. When you begin to see more and more plausible futures, your imagination runs wild with possibilities. Because scenarios are not future predictions of what will be, captivating scenarios are provocative, challenging, and stimulating. From finding a cure for cancer, to providing running water and electricity in every village of a particular country, the possibilities are limitless.

A scenario is often told best when you have several competing, opposite, and/or positive and negative scenarios interlinked and shared together. One story has your foundation expanding one hundred fold in its finances, employment base, product line, knowledge power, and services. What if your foundation exponentially increased one hundred fold? By telling the story in great detail of what you would accomplish, those you would hire, and the impact you would make, scenarios help you to start thinking in visionary ways. On the other hand, another scenario has your foundation losing its financial resources in the stock market, which means laying off employees and losing your ability to effectively support other charities. What should you do as a philanthropic leader if that should happen? Do you have a clear vision of what it takes to continue making a significant difference with few remaining resources? These questions come from implementing scenario workshops and brainstorming sessions with your leadership team, your foundation, or even your family. By getting others involved with possible stories of plausible futures, you are challenging assumptions, questioning your own strategic thinking, and adapting policies and procedures.

THE WHAT IF QUESTION

In 2000, the W. K. Kellogg Foundation and the David and Lucile Packard Foundation helped launch a new project called "The Future of Philanthropy." From this project came the "What If: The Art of Scenario Thinking for Nonprofits."[67] By asking the "what if" question, scenario thinking explores new areas of philanthropy. What if you increased your manpower by ten fold? What if you lost your ability to financially fund charities? What would you do? Would you continue as a philanthropic leader? What if you could increase the amount of people you serve with less? How might you go about doing it? These questions, as you can see, lead to many more questions. And questions are key to understanding the future and adapting accordingly.

When tough times hit Norm and Mary Jo Lorentz, owners of Three Cousins Subs sandwich franchise in Racine, Wisconsin, they had to ask questions.[68] It was not so much a matter of if they would survive the recession, but how they would survive? By turning to nonprofit organizations like civic clubs and local churches, they offered their products at reduced rates in order for the civic clubs and churches to be able to resell their sandwiches as their own fundraising initiatives. This clever move increased the profits and visibility of Three Cousins, while generating cash flow for the nonprofit world. This type of thinking and partnership only came when strategic questions were asked.

B CORPORATIONS

Quickly emerging into the future of philanthropy are B Corporations. B Corporations are for-profit corporations that realize generating income for shareholders sometimes comes at the detriment to employees, company values, and the community in which they reside. The B Corporation, on the other hand, is purpose driven rather than profit driven. This distinction allows benefits to flow to all stakeholders, rather than a few shareholders. With the emergence of B Corporations, social entrepreneurs, capitalistic philanthropic initiatives, and other socially responsible "good" marketplace organizations can finally join hands to show the world that organizations can be philanthropically sound, socially responsible, and purpose driven while generating income, keeping alignment with one's values, and making a difference in the world.

Since so many organizations today claim to "give back," be "green," or be an ethical and moral lighthouse in these dark days of Wall Street, B Corporations show, by their very nature, that they are held to a certain level of accountability, responsibility and standards. The instituting body that oversees B Corporations is a transparent 501 (c) 3 nonprofit, which understands the need for philanthropic leadership within the marketplace. Since so many business leaders desire to be more philanthropic within their organization, but simply cannot as a result of the bylaws and corporate governance of a typical C Corporation, the B Corporation empowers these philanthropic leaders, social entrepreneurs, and charitable business persons to live out their moral values and make a positive impact in the world in which they work. In order to understand the overall desire of B corporations, they declare the need for interdependence within the community, rather than independence. They hold the following truths:

- That we must be the change we seek in the world
- That all business ought to be conducted as if people and place mattered
- That, through their products, practices, and profits, businesses should aspire to do no harm and benefit all
- To do so requires that we act with the understanding that we are each dependent upon another and thus responsible for each other and future generations.[69]

SOCIAL BUSINESSES

In many ways social businesses are B Corporations, but traditionally they have not carried that title. The future of philanthropy may change this model, but for now social businesses are quickly gaining speed. A social business is also a cause-driven business that makes a profit for sustainability rather than wealth creation. And like traditional businesses, they must be self-sustainable or they will go out of business. Any initial capital given may be either written off as charity, or as a philanthropic investment, which the social business must pay back without interest. But once a social business is up and running, it basically has two options for using its profits. First, it can reinvest its profits in the business, by expanding into new markets, hiring more employees, investing in research and development, among other things. It cannot be used for a few executives to generate private wealth for themselves. Second, a social business may redistribute its profits in the form of shares to the poor where the business exists. This way the people who work within the social business and the community at large all benefit from the money it generates. An equal distribution of shares ensures that no one person takes over the social business and then converts it into a traditional for-profit enterprise.

In many ways, a social business is the future of philanthropy, because it is established on the values and principles of loving humankind in a participatory context. What this means is that the poor no longer need to live dependent, passive lives, but rather they can actively and collectively work to produce their own sustainability. Social businesses also contribute toward character development and relational development, while empowering each person to work from their strengths, skills, and knowledge. Because the goal is communal in focus, participatory in action, and social in outcomes, everyone gets an opportunity to engage in the process, while benefiting from the results. Unlike the traditional for-profit business, where only those at the top or those who received a special initial public offering become wealthy, all of the participants in a social business have the opportunity to grow and experience wealth beyond the type of greed a traditional business model may generate.

A New World of Philanthropy

With the rise of social businesses, B Corporations, and an infinite number of scenarios on the future of philanthropy, a new world of philanthropy is emerging out of business thought. Ideas such as "performance philanthropy," "philanthropicapitalism," "global social investing," "high impact philanthropy," and "venture philanthropy" all point to a new movement of philanthropic thought, whereby for-profit business ideas drive this multi-billion dollar industry. For instance:

The Gates Foundation, Sir John Templeton and the
Templeton Foundation ... invest in any initiative that
generates the results they seek, not just in nonprofits.
These philanthropists and many others have begun to see
philanthropy as a capital market. They demand the same
levels of transparency and accountability they expect from
stock markets.[70]

When applying business strategies from the market place of ideas,
philanthropic organizations are beginning to be run, managed and led as
businesses that measure results. By giving wisely, investing with intelligence,
and holding charities accountable, high-impact philanthropists desire to
make the biggest return on their gift as possible. Just as an investor in
the stock market examines the performance of their portfolio, likewise
you must treat your gifting in the same way. As the theoretical side of
philanthropy moves into the business realm of thinking, Opportunity
International implements these ideas as a case example.

In 2006, I met Dabbs Cavin in Kigali, Rwanda. Mr. Cavin works
for Opportunity International, a commercial bank targeting the poor in
Rwanda. This organization not only provides micro-business loans, savings,
and insurance products, it also inspires hope for the eighty-five percent of
the population living on less than $2 a day. The insurance products will
"help alleviate the impact of HIV/AIDS" as it provides more than 250,000
people with health benefits, claimed Cavin. The expected benefits over
the next five years are the creation of newly learned leadership skills and
financial education—not to mention the expected $8 million boost to
Rwanda's economy. Whatever future you choose, by allowing innovative,
wise business sense you can be the difference in the lives of others.

From micro-financing groups, like Kiva.org, to my niece living in
Accra, Ghana, teaching children art while serving in an orphanage, the
possibilities to exercise your philanthropic leadership are endless. Be it
in your local church or your community of neighbors, your leadership is
needed to bring innovation, ideas and insight to the world of philanthropy.
As you begin to live the philanthropic life, remember the future is yours
to shape, impact, and give into.

LEADERSHIP EXERCISE

Spend a few hours coming up with five to six different scenarios of the future of philanthropy. Create one or two scenarios for a conventional future, a counter future, and a creative future.

Since you have completed reading this book and working through the exercises, your next challenge is to become a philanthropic leader. Use this book as a reference for your own leadership journey.

- Make a list of ten people who need to read this book.
- Be philanthropic by giving this book to your friends.
- Start your own philanthropic leadership dialogue club.
- Discuss with others what you learn along the journey.

Conclusion

Philanthropy is harder than business. You are tackling
important problems that people with intellect and money
have tackled in the past and had a tough time solving.
—Warren Buffett

THROUGHOUT THE HISTORY OF HUMANITY, philosophers from Aristotle to businessmen like Warren Buffett understand the difficulties, challenges, and complexities surrounding philanthropy and the charitable spirit. Yes, it is easy to give money away, but philanthropy is about so much more than casting money to the wind. In order to make a positive, transformative, and lasting difference in the life of another person, you must understand that philanthropic leadership entails "investing in people—not giving to charity."[71] In order to maintain quality relationships, you first need to be willing to change yourself. This requires self-discipline, awareness, and personal leadership. After personally going through the grind of philanthropy and being refined by the fires of giving you will reach a place where you will reach out and bless another soul on his or her philanthropic journey. This of course requires time, and more importantly leadership.

Leadership is often a lonely road where the leader first steps into the darkness of the unknown before he or she personally takes others there. Often, philanthropic leadership entails the understanding that "giving blindly perpetuates the status quo of poverty in the world."[72] And the road is lonely because everyone wants your money without accountability. The road that many philanthropists and donors have gone down is the road where no accountability, feedback, or real measureable results exist. Because philanthropic leadership is different, you must be different as well. Your leadership will look different, feel different, and ultimately be different. Your giving habits will most likely change, and your ability to discern the deeper complexities and challenges will mature from having once been a drive-by giver to now being a wise philanthropic leader.

Therefore, today's philanthropic leadership requires a well thought out strategy grounded in truth, established on love, centered on people, and pointed toward the future. This leadership takes time, humility, a teachable spirit, and a pursuit for credible feedback. As you gather results from followers, programs, and funding philanthropic endeavors, both quantitative and qualitative measures will better inform your strategic decisions. As a result, when you commit to living out your principles, beliefs, and values and personally align them with your philanthropic work, then you will be in a better position to serve, love others, and lead a difference into the future. If you produce more donor followers, as you model the way, inspire a shared vision, challenge the process, enable others to act, and encourage the heart, then these leaders should transform into philanthropic leaders as well.

As you take on a spirit of social entrepreneurship by thinking outside the box, continue to aim for a maximum return on your investment. Let yourself be transformed by the process, as you love others from where they are. As you listen, learn, and liberate the lives of others, remember philanthropy is not solely about money, but rather about investing in the lives of people. As Gandhi proposed over fifty years ago, so too his question continues to challenge each of us today:

> Recall the face of the poorest and weakest man whom you
> may have seen, and ask yourself if the step you contemplate
> is going to be of any use to him. Will he gain anything by

it? Will it restore him to a control over his own life and destiny? In other words, will it lead to freedom for the hungry and spiritually starving millions?[73]

Source Notes

T HE SOURCES FROM THIS BOOK come from many interviews and real world experience from working with private foundations to public charities. My personal travels from places like Africa to Haiti bring robust, first-hand research to this project as well. The quotes under each chapter and section are available from www.brainyquote.com. I have also drawn from the following:

Badaracco, Joseph L. "The Discipline of Building Character." *Harvard Business Review*, March–April 1998.

Banjo, Shelly. "Small Business Give—And Get Back—From Their Community." *The Wall Street Journal Online* Available from http:// blogs.wsj.com/independentstreet/2008/11/26/small-businesses-give- and-get-backfrom-their-community/. Internet; accessed 1 December 2008.

Bekker, Corne. "The Philippians Hymn (2:5–11) as an early mimetic Christological model of Christian Leadership in Roman Philippi." Servant Leadership Research Roundtable. Virginia Beach: Regent

University, August 2006.

Bennis, Warren. "The End of Leadership: Exemplary Leadership is Impossible Without Full Inclusion, Initiatives, and Cooperation of Followers." *Organizational Dynamics*, 1999, 71–79.

Berresford, Susan V. "American Philanthropic Values and the Future of Philanthropy." Remarks by Susan V. Berresford at the New York Region Association of Grantmakers Annuel Meeting, 11 May 1999, New York Public Library. Available from http://www.fordfound.org/newsroom/speeches/108. Internet; accessed 9 December 2007.

Bishop, Matthew and Michael Green. *Philanthro-Capitalism: How The Rich Can Save the World*. New York: Bloomsbury Press, 2008.

Brookshire, M. S. "Virtue Ethics and Servant Leadership." *Ethic News & Views*. Atlanta: Center for Ethics, Emory University, April 1, 2001.

Buckingham, Marcus and Donald O. Clifton. *Now, Discover Your Strengths*. New York: The Free Press, 2001.

Center for High Impact Philanthropy. "What Is High Impact Philanthropy?" Philadelphia: University of Pennsylvania. Available from http://www.impact.upenn.edu/our_work/documents/WhatisHighImpactPhilanthropy_initialconceptpaperApril2007_000.pdf. Internet; accessed 24 April 2007.

Clinton, Bill. *Giving: How Each of Us Can Change the World*. New York: Knopf, 2007.

Collins, Jim. *Good to Great and the Social Sectors: Why Business Thinking is Not the Answer*. New York: HarperCollins, 2005.

Collins, Jim. *Good to Great: Why Some Companies Make the Leap and Other Don□t*. New York: Harper Business, 2001.

Covey, Stephen R. *The 7 Habits of Highly Effective People: Restoring the*

Character Ethic. New York: Fireside, 1989.

Donaldson, Thomas. "Values in Tension: Ethics Away from Home." *Harvard Business Review on Corporate Ethics.* Boston: Harvard Business School Press, 2003.

Easterly, William. *The White Man's Burden: Why the West's Efforts to Aid the Rest have Done so Much Ill and so Little Good.* New York: Penguin, 2006.

Elmer, Duane. *Cross-Cultural Conflict: Building Relationships for Effective Ministry.* Downers Grove, IL: InterVarsity Press, 1993.

Fals-Borda, Orlando and Muhammad Anisur Rahman. *Action and Knowledge: Breaking the Monopoly with Participatory Action Research.* New York: Intermediate Technology Publications/Apex Press. 1991.

Ferguson, Everett. *Background of Early Christianity*. 2nd ed. Grand Rapids: Eerdmans Publishing, 1993.

Friedman, Stewart D. *Total Leadership: Be a Better Leader, Have a Richer Life.* Boston: Harvard Business Press, 2008.

Fulton, Katherine and Andrew Blau. "Imagining the Future of Philanthropy: Looking Back from 2025." *The Future of Philanthropy*, Available from, http://www.futureofphilanthropy.org/files/philTom_1ImaginingFuture.pdf. Internet.

Gates, Bill. "Bill Gates: The Way We Give." *Fortune*, 9 January 2007. Available from http://money.cnn.com/2007/01/09/magazines/fortune/Gates_philanthropy.fortune/index.htm. Internet; accessed 15 September 2007.

Gilmore, James H., and B. Joseph Pine. *Authenticity: What Consumers Really Want.* Boston: Harvard Business School Press, 2007.

Goffee, Rob and Gareth Jones. *Why Should Anyone Be Led by You? What it*

Takes to Be an Authentic Leader. Boston: Harvard Business School Press, 2006.

Goleman, Daniel. *Emotional Intelligence: Why it Can Matter More than IQ*. New York:Bantom, 1995.

Greenleaf, Robert. *The Servant as Leader*. Indianapolis: The Robert Greenleaf Center, 1970.

Guinness, Os. *The Call: Finding and Fulfilling The Central Purpose of Your Life*. Nashville: Word, 1998.

Handy, Charles. "What's A Business For." *Harvard Business Review on Corporate Responsibility*. Boston: Harvard Business School Press, 2003.

Healy, B. "Foundations veer into Charity." *The Boston Globe*. Available fromhttp://www.boston.com/news/nation/articles/2003/12/03/ foundations_veer_into_business/. Internet; accessed 3 December 2003.

Hesselbein, Frances. "Venture Philanthropy: Investing in People—Not Giving to Charity." Available from http://media.wiley.com/ assets/45/41/0787958018_Hesselbein.pdf. Internet; accessed 10 November 2009.

Hines, Andy. "Strategic Foresight." Bethesda, MD: World Future Society, 2006.

Hines, Andy and Peter Bishop. *Thinking About the Future: Guidelines for Strategic Foresight*. Washington, DC: Social Technologies, 2006.

Iacocca, Lee. *Where Have All the Leaders Gone?* New York: Scribner, 2007.

Keidel, Robert W. *Seeing Organizational Patterns: A New Theory and Language of Organizational Design*. Washington, D.C.: Beard Books, 1995.

Kellerman, Barbara. *Followership: How Followers Are Creating Change and Changing Leaders*. Boston: Harvard Business Press, 2008.

Kiel, Fred and Doug Lennick. *Moral Intelligence: Enhancing Business Performance and Leadership Success*. Upper Saddle River, New Jersey: Wharton School Publishing, 2005.

Kouzes, James M. and Barry Z. Posner. *Leadership Practices Inventory: Participant's Workbook*. 3rd Ed. San Francisco: Pfeiffer, 2003.

Kouzes, James M., and Barry Z. Posner. *Credibility: How Leaders Gain and Lose It, Why People Demand It*. San Francisco: Jossey-Bass, 1993.

Korngold, Alice. *Leveraging Good Will: Strengthening Nonprofits by Engaging Businesses*. San Francisco: Jossey-Bass, 2005.

Laney, Marti Olsen. *The Introvert Advantage*. New York: Workman Publishing, 2002.

Lincoln, Yvonna S. and Egon G. Guba, "Paradigmatic Controversies, Contradictions, and Emerging Confluences." In Norman K. Denzin and Yvonna S. Lincoln (Eds.), *Handbook of Qualitative Research*. London: Sage, 2000.

Lumarada, Joe. "Philanthropy, Self-Fulfillment, and the Leadership of Community Foundations." *Leader to Leader*. No. 22 Fall 2001. Available from http://www.leadertoleader.org/knowledgecenter/journal.aspx?ArticleID=113. Internet; accessed 20 June 2007.

Malphurs, Aubrey. *Values-Driven Leadership: Discovering and Developing Your Core Values for Ministry*. Grand Rapids: Baker Books, 2004.

Martin, Maximilian. "Taking a Structured Approach to Your Giving." UBS Philanthropy Services. Available from, http://www.philanthropycapital.org/Newsletter/Summer06/UBS.html. Internet; accessed Summer 2006.

Mitchell, Stephen. *Tao Te Ching: A New English Version*. New York: Harper Perennial, 2006.

Monitor Company Group, LLP. "Scenarios: The Pressure of Accountability." Available from http://www.futureofphilanthropy.org/files/philTom_2ThePressure.pdf. Internet; accessed 2005.

Nadler, David A., and Michael L. Tushman. *Competing by Design: The Power of Organizational Architecture.* Oxford: Oxford University Press, 1997.

Nash, Laura and Howard Stevenson. *Just Enough: Tools for Creating Success in Your Work and Life*. New Jersey: John Wiley and Sons, 2004.

Nash, Ronald H. *Life's Ultimate Questions: An Introductory to Philosophy*. Grand Rapids: Zondervan, 1999.

Nobel, Trevor. *Social Theory and Social Change*. New York: Palgrave, 2000.

Patterson, Kathleen. "Servant Leadership: A Theoretical Model." Presented at Servant Leadership Research Roundtable, Virginia Beach, Virginia, August 2004.

Pfeffer, Jeffrey. *The Human Equation: Building Profits by Putting People First.* Boston: Harvard Business School Press, 1998.

Plato. *Euthyphro, Apology, Crito* (F. J. Church, Trans.). Indianapolis: The Bobbs-Merrill Company, 1956.

Porter, Michael E., and Mark R. Kramer. "The Competitive Advantage of Corporate Philanthropy." *Harvard Business Review*, 1 December 2002.

Raguin, Y. *I am Sending You (John 22:21): Spirituality of the Missioner*. Manila: East Asian Pastoral Institute, 1973.

Raymond, Susan U. *The Future of Philanthropy: Economics, Ethics, and*

Management. Hoboken: Wiley, 2004.

Reason, Peter and Hillary Bradbury. *Handbook of Action Research*. London: Saga, 2006.

Reason, Peter. "A Participatory Worldview." Available from http://people. bath.ac.uk.mnspwr/Papers/Participatoryworld.htm. Internet; accessed 26 February 2008.

Reason, Peter. "Three Approaches to Participative Inquiry." Available from http://people.bath.ac.uk/mnspwr/Papers/YVONNA.htm. Internet; accessed 26 February 2008.

Rokeach, Milton. *Understanding Human Values: Individual and Societal*. New York: Free Press, 1979.

Sachs, Jeffrey D. *The End of Poverty: Economic Possibilities for Our Time*. New York: Penguin Books, 2006.

Schervish, Paul. "What Sustains Donors During the Current Climate?" An essay given at Boston College, 9 June 2009.

Schroeder, Alice. *Warren Buffett and the Business of Life*. New York: Bantam, 2008.

Schwartz, Peter. *The Art of the Long View: Planning for the Future in an Uncertain World*. New York: Doubleday, 1991.

Senge, Peter M. *The Fifth Discipline: The Art & Practice of the Learning Organization*. New York: Doubleday Currency, 1990.

Silverman, Rachel Emma. "A New Generation Reinvents Philanthropy." *The Wall Street Journal Online*, 21 August 2007. Available from http:// online.wsj.com/public/ article/SB118765256378003494.html. Internet; accessed 15 September 2007.

Slaughter, Richard. "Foresight and Philanthropy—Towards a New Alliance." Brisbane: Foresight International. Available from: http://foresightinternational.com.au/catalogue/resources/Fsight_Philanthropy_Intro.pdf. Internet; accessed June 2005.

Smith, Bucklin and Associates. *The Complete Guide to Nonprofit Management.* ed.

Robert H. Wilbur. 2nd ed. New York: Wiley, 2000.

Spears, Larry. *Insights on Leadership.* New York: Wiley & Sons, 1998.

Stearns, Richard. *The Hole in Our Gospel: The Answers that Changed My Life and Might Just Change the World.* Nashville: Thomas Nelson, 2009.

Stein, Steven J. and Howard E. Book. *The EQ Edge: Emotional Intelligence and Your Success.* Toronto: Multi-Health Systems, 2000.

Stossel, John and Kristina Kendall. "Who Gives and Who Doesn't? Putting the Stereotypes to the Test." 28, November 2006. *ABC News.* Available from http://abcnews.go.com/2020/story?id=2682730&page=1&page=1. Internet; accessed 15 September 2007.

Thall, Bill, Bruce McNicol and John Lynch. *True Faced: Trust God and Others with Who You Really Are.* Colorado Springs: NavPress, 2003.

Thurman, Eric. "Performance Philanthropy: Bringing Accountability to Charitable Giving." *Harvard International Review* no. 1, vol. XXXVIII, (Spring 2006): 18–20.

U2. "Numb (Give Me Some More Dignity Mix)." *U2 The Best of 1990–2000.* Universal Music International, 2000.

Victor, Philip. "Starbucks Wasting More Than 6 Million Gallons of Water a Day: Amount of Water Lost Is Enough to Fill an

Olympic Pool Every 83 Minutes." *ABC News*. 6 October 2008. Available from http://abcnews.go.com/International/SmartHome/ story?id=5964908&page=1. Internet.

Whiteman, D. L. "Anthropology and Mission: The Incarnational Connection." *Missiology* 31.4, 2003.

Yunus, Muhammad. *Creating a World Without Poverty: Social Business and the Future of Capitalism*. New York: Public Affairs, 2007.

Zweifel, Thomas D. *Cultural Clash: Managing the Global High-Performance Team*. New York: Select Books, 2003.

About the Author

STEVEN GRAY KELLER IS A philosopher, poet, and philanthropist. He has a Bachelor's degree in philosophy, a Master's degree in theology, and a Doctorate in leadership. Dr. Keller is the principal consultant at Intentional Solutions, a nontraditional think tank specializing in the study of spirituality, leadership, and philanthropy. He serves on several nonprofit boards, and currently presides over the Leader Foundation. He lives in Lake Nona, Florida, where he enjoys thinking and writing from his back porch.

Contact Information

To learn more about the thinking of Dr. Keller or to contact him for a workshop, consulting or speaking engagement, please see the following:

http://web.me.com/intentionalsolutions/Site/Home.html

http://twitter.com/perspectitude

http://intentionalsolutions.blogspot.com/

Notes

6. Eric Thurman, "Performance Philanthropy: Bringing Accountability to Charitable Giving," *Harvard International Review*, no 1 (Spring 2006): 18.

7. Muhammad Yunus, *Creating a World Without Poverty: Social Business and the Future of Capitalism* (New York: Public Affairs, 2007), 115.

8. CNBC, American Greed aired on Wednesday, March 6, 2010.

9. U2, "Numb (Give Me Some More Dignity Mix)." *U2 The Best of 1990–2000*. Universal Music International, 2000.

10. Paul Schervish, "What Sustains Donors During the Current Climate?" An essay delivered at Boston College, 9 June 2009.

11. Duane Elmer, *Cross-Culture Conflict: Building Relationships for Effective Ministry* (Downers Grove: InterVarsity Press, 1993), 156.

12. Larry Spears, *Insights on Leadership* (New York: Wiley & Sons, 1998), 4, 5.

13. Ibid.

14. Available from http://www.givewell.net; Internet.

15. Ronald H. Nash, *Life's Ultimate Questions: An Introductory to Philosophy* (Grand Rapids: Zondervan Publishing House), 25.

16. Ibid., 26.

17. Ibid.

18. Ibid., 27.

19. Ibid., 28.

20. Laura Nash and Howard Stevenson, *Just Enough: Tools for Creating Success in Your Work and Life* (New Jersey: John Wiley and Sons, 2004), 119.

21. Ibid.

22. Joseph Badaracco, "The Discipline of Building Character,"

Harvard Business Review, March–April 1998, 5–14.

23. Ibid., 5.

24. Ibid.

25. Peter Reason, "A Participatory Worldview"; Available from http://people.bath.ac.uk.mnspwr/Papers/Participatoryworld. htm; Internet; accessed 26 February 2008.

26. Ibid.

27. Peter Reason, "Three Approaches to Participative Inquiry," 6.

28. Ibid.

29. Yunus, *Creating a World Without Poverty*, 116.

30. D. L. Whiteman, "Anthropology and Mission: The Incarnational Connection," *Missiology*, 2003, 31.4, 397–415.

31. Peter Reason, *Three Approaches to Participative Inquiry*, 13.

32. Ibid.

33. William Easterly, *The White Man's Burden: Why the West's Efforts to Aid the Rest Have Done so Much Ill and so Little Good* (New York: The Penguin Press, 2006), 26.

34. Ibid., 17.

35. Yunus, 116.

36. Peter Reason, "Three Approaches to Participatory Inquiry" in N. K. Denzin & Y. S. Lincoln (Eds.), *Handbook of Qualitative Research* (Thousand Oaks: Sage, 1994), 324–339.

37. Yunus, 115.

38. Susan U. Raymond, *The Future of Philanthropy: Economics, Ethics, and Management* (Hoboken: Wiley, 2004), 25.

39. Ibid., 25, 26.

40. Yunus, 116.

41. Stephen Mitchell, *Tao Te Ching: A New English Version* (New York: Harper Perennial, 1988), 10.

42. Richard Stearns, *The Hole in Our Gospel: The Answers that Changed My Life and Might Just Change the World* (Nashville: Thomas Nelson, 2009), 130.

43. Alice Schroeder, *The Snowball: Warren Buffett and the Business of Life* (New York: Bantam Books, 2008), 816.

44. Rob Goffee and Gareth Jones, *Why Should Anyone Be Led by*

You? What It Takes to Be an Authentic Leader (Boston: Harvard Business School Press, 2006), 67.

45. James M. Kouzes and Barry Z. Posner, *Leadership Practices Inventory* (San Francisco: Pfeiffer, 2003), 11, 12.

46. Quentin Hardy, "Hope and Profit in Africa: How do you build consumer markets and fight AIDS in a broken land? MTV banks on music videos and local talent," *Forbes* 179, no. 13 (18 June 2007): 94.

47. Ibid., 96.

48. Jim Collins, *Good to Great and the Social Sectors* (New York: HarperCollins, 2005), 5.

49. Ibid., 8.

50. Eric Thurman, "Performance Philanthropy," 19.

51. Ibid.

52. Ibid.

53. Ibid.

54. Ibid., 20.

55. William Easterly, *The White Man's Burden*, 15, 16.

56. Center for High Impact Philanthropy, "What Is High Impact Philanthropy?" Philadelphia: University of Pennsylvania, 24 April 2007; Available from http://www.impact.upenn.edu/ our_work/documents/WhatisHighImpactPhilanthropy_ initialconceptpaperApril2007_000.pdf; Internet.

57. Ibid.

58. Laura Nash and Howard Stevenson, *Just Enough*, 82.

59. Steven J. Stein and Howard E. Book, *The EQ Edge: Emotional Intelligence and Your Success* (Toronto: Multi-Health Systems, 2000), 111.

60. Stewart D. Friedman, *Total Leadership: Be a Better Leader, Have a Better Life* (Boston: Harvard Business School Publishing, 2008), 10.

61. Warren Bennis, "The End of Leadership: Exemplary Leadership Is Impossible Without Full Inclusion, Initiatives, and Cooperation of Followers," *Organizational Dynamics*, 1997, 71–79.

62. Charles Handy, "What's A Business For," *Harvard Business*

Review on Corporate Responsibility (Boston: Harvard Business School Press, 2003), 67.

63. Rob Goffee and Gareth Jones, *Why Should Anyone Be Led by You*, 9.

64. Jim Collins, *Good to Great: Why Some Companies Make the Leap and Others Don't* (New York: Harper Business, 2001), 42.

65. Everett Ferguson, *Backgrounds of Early Christianity* 2nd ed. (Grand Rapids: William B. Eerdmans Publishing Co., 1993), 110.

66. Robert Greenleaf, *The Servant As Leader* (Indianapolis: The Robert Greenleaf Center, 1970), 7.

67. Stephen R. Covey, *The 7 Habits of Highly Effective People: Powerful Lessons in Personal Change* (New York: Fireside, Simon & Schuster, 1989), 195.

68. Available from http://www.ethoswater.com.

69. Philip Victor, "Starbucks Wasting More Than 6 Million Gallons of Water a Day: Amount of Water Lost Is Enough to Fill an Olympic Pool Every 83 Minutes," *ABC News* 6 October 2008; Available from http://abcnews.go.com/International/ SmartHome/story?id=5964908&page=1; Internet.

70. Ibid.

71. Yunus, 240.

72. Diana Scearce, Katherine Fulton, and the Global Business Network community, "What If? The Art of Scenario Thinking for Nonprofits," Global Business Network, a member of the Monitor Group; Available from http://www.gbn.com/articles/ pdfs/ GBN_What%20If.pdf; Internet; accessed 2004.

73. Banjo Shelly, *Wall Street Journal Blogs*, "Small Businesses Give—And Get Back—From Their Community"; available from Wall Street Journal Blogs, from http://blogs.wsj.com/ independentstreet/2008/11/26/small-businesses-give-and-get-backfrom-their-community/; Internet; accessed 26 November 2008.

74. Available from http://www.bcorporation.net/declaration; Internet.

75. Thurman, 19.
76. Frances Hesselbein, "Venture Philanthropy: Investing in People—Not Giving to Charity"; Available from http://media.wiley.com/assets/45/41/0787958018_Hesselbein.pdf; Internet; accessed 19 June 2007.
77. Ibid., 20.
78. Gandhi quoted in Thomas D. Zweifel, *Culture Clash: Managing the Global High- Performance Team* (New York: Select Books, 2003), xxvii.

CPSIA information can be obtained at www.ICGtesting.com
Printed in the USA

236573LV00001B/2/P